the BATTLE WAS NOT Mine

JANICE CODLING

CONCLUSIO
HOUSE PUBLISHING

Copyright © 2017 by Janice Codling

All rights reserved. This book or any portion thereof may not be reproduced or used in any manner whatsoever without the express written permission of the publisher except for the use of brief quotations in a book review.

"The Battle Was Not Mine"
REL099000: RELIGION / Christian Life / Spiritual Warfare
BIO018000: Biography & Autobiography/Religious

Printed in Canada
First Printing, 2017

ISBN 978-0-9949204-9-2

Published by:
Conclusio House Publishing
503-7700 Hurontario Street
Suite 209
Brampton, ON
L6Y 4M3

www.conclusiohouse.com

Scripture quotations taken from the Amplified® Bible (AMP), Copyright © 2015 by The Lockman Foundation
Used by permission. www.Lockman.org

THE HOLY BIBLE, NEW INTERNATIONAL VERSION®, NIV®
Copyright © 1973, 1978, 1984, 2011 by Biblica, Inc.® Used by permission. All rights reserved worldwide.

Scripture quotations marked (NLT) are taken from the Holy Bible, New Living Translation, copyright © 1996, 2004, 2007 by Tyndale House Foundation. Used by permission of Tyndale House Publishers, Inc., Carol Stream, Illinois 60188. All rights reserved.

This book is dedicated to the One who always provides, supplies, covers and protects, who is a keeper when I shouldn't have been kept, who is my safety net, my lover, my Saviour, my best friend, my strong tower, my healer, the great physician in my sick room, my lawyer in times of trouble, my peace in the midst of every storm, my shield that hides me in times when shame and mere embarrassment should have captured and devoured me, but most importantly, He is my source of life and survival. And for that, I dedicate this book to Jesus Christ, our soon and coming King and our God.

Without you, God, this book would not have been possible. Thank you for the numerous revelations and confirmations through visions, dreams, and your chosen people that you sent to me through the prophetic to encourage me to finish this book that absolutely no one knew about, except you. This book is dedicated to you, because you protected and saved me from all that is written in this book. The words 'thank you' are an understatement. This is for you, God! Thank you, and I love you!

ACKNOWLEDGMENTS

The following people deserve to be acknowledged for pushing me, praying with me, and motivating me to complete this book. Without these people, I don't think finishing would've been possible. Thank you for your patience, for your time, and for pouring into my life during this season. God's richest blessings to you!

Maxford Codling (R.I.P. father), Yvonne Codling (mother), Denese Codling (sister), Levar Sterling (cousin), Melissa & Otis Nunes (sister & brother), Alisa Falconer (god-sister), Treva Ryan (friend), Monique Gunnis (friend), Keith Hill (friend), Vivika Green (friend), Andre Gordon (friend), Angelica Cole (friend), Thessalonica Thomas (friend), Sheliza Soochit (friend), Pastor Caleen Howard, Apostle Jeremy & First Lady Banks, Bishop Wayne Channer, Pastor Robin Albright, Bishop Oneil & First Lady Walker, Apostle G. Irvin, Gary Baptiste, Kris Archer, Darvelle Hutchins, Pastor Richard Mckenzie, and Kerri-Ann Haye-Donawa (publisher).

INTRODUCTION

Even with my strong spiritual desire to write this book, it didn't dawn on me that you could be healed through the words of your testimony. Not only can you be healed and set free, but the power that dwells within you allows your story to heal someone else. Like I said, I always thought of writing my own book to help somebody, even if it was just one person. You may ask, "Why?" Well, I once heard a good friend of mine say, "Your story has the ability to bring healing, both to the reader and to the writer." So at all costs, without a shadow of a doubt, I've written this book to not only introduce you to the creativity inside of me but also to do the words of Revelation 12:11—"And they overcame him (the devil) by the blood of the Lamb, and by the word of their testimony; and they did not love their lives to death."

It was with great meditation, prayer, and supplication that I strategically wrote this book. Every day, as I would prepare myself to write and add to each chapter, I thought about you. You reading this book, whether you are female or male, I asked God the Creator to help me put something in this book that you could relate to. And even if you cannot relate to it, my prayer was that everyone who lays their hands on this book would be blessed beyond measure and filled with power and might to approach life, again.

This book was written from a pure place located inside my heart. The purpose of this book is to let you know that until you answer God's call that is ringing on the inside of your heart, He will continue to call you. In other words, until you really follow what is dearest to your heart concerning your walk with God—the visions, the dreams, the aspirations and, most importantly, what and who you are called to be in Jesus—know that He, the Lord God, will continue to call you until He gets your attention.

Throughout this book you will see scriptures from the Bible. These scriptures will help me throughout each chapter to get my point across for you to understand where I am coming from and, most importantly, for you to freely examine your life and see how valuable you are to Jesus Christ. With that being said, I personally did not know how valuable I was to God. Therefore, every encounter I had with people who walked heavily in the prophetic anointing, I wondered why God would always want to locate me and give me warning after warning, or even just confirm the many hidden petitions and requests I held onto in my heart. In all honesty, confirmations are not a coincidence; they were designed long before you or I could comprehend what the word means. So, I believe confirmation is God's way of letting us know that our prayers have been answered.

If you're reading this book in hopes of receiving help with taking risks in the midst of a struggle, look no further. This book is just an example of how God can place His hand upon your life, without you even knowing it, without you even knowing He could take the stormy situations of life and turn them into bright rays of sunshine. With grace and peace, I urge you to embark on this journey that the Lord has allowed me to release on His behalf in hopes of winning souls into His Kingdom, the Body of Jesus Christ.

The BATTLE WAS NOT Mine

Table of Contents

CHAPTER 1	Unforeseen Purpose	1
CHAPTER 2	Bullying Almost Buried Me	12
CHAPTER 3	Reflecting on My Rejection	22
CHAPTER 4	The Wilderness Experience	32
CHAPTER 5	Broken to Peace	43
CHAPTER 6	The Revolving Door: Matters of the Heart	54
CHAPTER 7	The Black Sheep Experience: The Misfit	64
CHAPTER 8	A.K.A.WOG	73
CHAPTER 9	Secretly Bruised Behind Ministry	86
CHAPTER 10	Leave the Boat	96
CHAPTER 11	The Battle Is For His Glory	104
CHAPTER 12	The Best Is Yet to Come	111

CHAPTER 1

Unforeseen Purpose

"It's a girl!" Those are the words I imagine my mother and father heard when the doctor slapped me on the butt when I entered this world. Not only was this a blessing to both my parents, but this was my expected time of arrival. On January 3, 1988, at North Western General Hospital in Toronto, Ontario, God stretched forth His hand and performed a miracle. Now, many may be wondering what I could possibly mean by a "miracle," and if I even know what the word means. According to Dictionary.com, a miracle is "an effect or extraordinary event in the physical world that surpasses all known human or natural powers and is ascribed to a supernatural cause."

Hello, my name is Janice Codling, and I am a miracle. You're about to embark on a journey, a journey that was filled with pain, hurt, brokenness, anger, defeat, rejection, along with many signs and wonders. You see, it was said to me that every time I shared my story, or in this case my testimony, about when I was born and how I was born, many would say things like, "Wow! Janice, you truly are a miracle." Now, even though many people would call my entire conception a miracle, I see myself as a miracle from God. Miraculously, God showed up on my behalf inside my mother's womb. While tucked away inside my mother's womb, He knew me. He allowed my birth to be the reason why I have no choice in the matter but to serve Him. God surely had a unique way of bringing me into existence as a premature baby, a child that had a purpose drawn up by the Creator and written before conception. It was with great diligence that I took it upon myself to study the meaning of being born prematurely, because growing up I just heard my mother and the rest of my family say how much of a miracle I was, but I had no understanding of what God truly did for me. As I studied this part of my life, I learned that a premature or preterm birth is the birth of a baby before the organs are mature enough to allow normal survival after birth. You can only imagine how shocked I was to learn this information about myself.

Just to think that God would have kept someone like me, appointed for such a time as this, baffles me. Shockingly, I was born at just seven months; a full-term pregnancy is a full nine months. But this wasn't even the miraculous part of my birth; it was only the brink of what God was truly about to do in my life. The Bible says in Jeremiah 1:5 that *"Before I formed you in the womb I knew (and) approved of you [as my chosen instrument], and before you were born I separated and set you apart, consecrating you: [and] I appointed you as a prophet to the nations"* (AMP). Believe that the Lord had us in mind, even before you and I were created. He already knew what He wanted us to be and how He wanted us to look before we even knew ourselves. So for me, it would be safe to say that God knew me before I was yet conceived in my mother's precious womb.

God is like a potter, and each of us is like clay. "A potter is someone who creates pottery; the potter creates this work of art with clay. Clay is earthly material, almost like mud."[1] It is written in the Holy Scriptures that God is the Potter, and we are the clay. The job of the potter is to create that which he desires out of the clay (Isaiah 64:8). So even when we make our own plans and our own decisions, know that God works in mysterious ways, making sure He puts our feet back on track in order for us to reach our purpose, which is His perfect will.

---

1 https://answersingenesis.org/human-body/from-dust-to-dust/

The birthing process is one that takes time, and I can only imagine how my mother must've felt when it came time to give birth to me. My mother would often remind me of the process she had to go through, the excruciating pain, and the aftermath of giving birth. The part that I hold on to ever so dearly is that at birth I weighed only one pound, twelve ounces. Yes! One pound! Now, learning this truly puzzled me, and even being the age that I am right now, I still can't believe that God would save me from death, at birth. I'll never begin to comprehend the ways of God, because He works in mysterious ways. There are countless times that I have sat and meditated on my life, and as far as I can remember, I am always reminded that God truly has a purpose for me, and He surely has a purpose for you as well. No matter how impossible things may look to you, He is in control.

If you have gotten this far in the book, I just want to thank God for your life. The title of this chapter is Unforeseen Purpose. The word unforeseen, according to the Webster's Dictionary, means "being unexpected, sudden, unanticipated or emergent." I did not realize the extent of the purpose over my life, some of which I just could not see. Sometimes God had to perform certain signs and wonders to grab hold of my attention to let me know that He is in control of my life. Oftentimes in life, we tend to want what we want, whether it is in secret or it is out in the public. We tend to plan our lives according to what we want and not based on what we truly need. Surely, at some point in your life you've planned your life according to what you felt would allow you to 'get rich quick.' I sure know I did. But as I began to grow up and then grow in Jesus Christ, I realized that *purpose* over *money* is what would get me to God's perfect will for my life.

I asked the Lord, numerous times, what He desired for me to do or be on His behalf and, realistically, I would always try to stay in tune with His voice. But sometimes I just wanted my own way, I just wanted to be my own person and abide by no rules whatsoever. Have you ever had those feelings? Wanting your own way but knowing that you just can't have it because God has a purpose and a call on your life and, at some point, He will redirect your footsteps without you even knowing it. Well, the Bible says in Proverbs 16:9, *"In their hearts humans plan their course, but the LORD establishes their steps."* So even though I planned my own life—the way I chose to do it—at the end of the day, the Lord God Himself redirected my footsteps on to His pathway and for His righteousness.

So, once again, before you and I were even created inside the womb of our mothers, God had us in mind and knew exactly who and what we would become. In other words, He has the master plan. Grace and mercy kept me in the form of a miracle, and although at times I wonder why God would do all of this for me, He constantly reminds me that He loves me. I can recall my mother telling me stories about the many challenges I had when I was born; things like breathing on my own due to being born prematurely and being so small. It was at this time in my infancy that doctors told my mother that I would need to have an important procedure done. This procedure was called a *tracheotomy,* and this was to be done in the middle of my throat. A tracheotomy or tracheostomy is "an opening surgically created through the neck into the trachea (windpipe) to allow direct access to the breathing tube and is commonly done in an operating room under general anesthesia."[2] This procedure usually takes place when the airway is obstructed, in order to clean and remove secretions from the airway, and as a way to supply oxygen safely to the lungs. Due to the fact that I was unable to breathe on my own because my lungs were too small, the tracheotomy was done for me as a way to supply oxygen to my lungs. Even through this, I had no idea God had a divine purpose and a plan for me. Not being able to breathe on my own at birth was probably a big deal for both my parents, though to me it was unknown. But God! God knew that in order to

---

2 http://www.mayoclinic.org/tests-procedures/tracheostomy/details/what-you-can-expect/rec-20234018

bring about His glory and His work in my life, He had to give me a story. You see, that is what God does for His people. We all have a story that He has given us to help impact others who miss His very existence. So it is our stories that help us uplift, encourage, and motivate those around us. Our stories have the ability to save someone who's about to go through the same thing you or I have already gone through.

God is a God who works in mysterious ways, ways in which we will never understand, because if we began to understand Him, then we would not have a need to call upon Him. And when we act as if we don't need Him, we become our own gods to ourselves. So, what is unforeseen to you and me was already premeditated in God's thoughts, and all that was left for Him to do was to bring us into existence. My life at birth is a prime example that God truly does exist and that miracles do happen. But not only that, I believe that God wanted me to be alive so that I could write this chapter of my life and then turn around and share it with His people, both lost and saved. I strongly believe that not only will it give people hope, but it will also give them a voice to speak up and share their testimonies. My unforeseen purpose was designed by God for this time and for this very reason.

I can remember, very clearly, my mother telling me on every birthday as I got older, "Janice, I remember when you were so little I could hold you in just one palm. But look at how big you have gotten, and so fast!"

Sometimes you can only go off of what others could see in a situation such as this one. But I gave that example because it goes to show you, and even me, that when God has a purpose for your life, even though you can't see it, He does. In other words, when God chooses you and appoints you for a specific thing or a specific call, He doesn't just call you because you look the part; He calls you because He looks at your heart. The Bible says in 1 Samuel 16:7, *"But the Lord said to Samuel, 'Don't judge by his appearance or height, for I have rejected him. The Lord doesn't see things the way you see them. People judge by outward appearance, but the Lord looks at the heart.'"* This scripture demonstrates that although we, as humans, may look at the outward appearance of a person, God looks at the heart.

Throughout my entire life, as I grew, I experienced things that caused me to perform lowly and not in my divine purpose. My life has always been a mystery from birth to present, with many twist and turns, near death experiences and evil distractions. But one thing that I can truly say is that the Lord has been my Saviour, protector, provider, doctor, lawyer and, most of all, Father. Not to sound too spiritual, but this part of my testimony would not have been possible without Him, because I would not be here to testify to you if it had not been for Him. Not many premature babies survive a one-pound testimony such as mine, especially one who could not breathe on her own, one who struggled to be able to eat. But God, God had a different plan, and He saved me for such a time as this, and for this I am thankful.

My purpose was not always clear to me, but as I got older, my prayers were for God to reveal His will to me. Why? Because once I realized that absolutely no one would be able to help me and care for me like He would, I wanted to be deeply connected to Him and to have a close relationship with Him. From the very beginning of my life, God's will was to preserve me for such a time as this. He saw in me a heart that wanted to live, eat of His Word, breathe, and walk in His will for my life. At times, we tend to want to know the finished product before it is actually finished, but how is that possible? Life is like baking a cake. You need all the right ingredients to go into the cake so that it comes out tasting good. When you add something that is not listed in the recipe, the cake may come out tasting awful. Likewise, when we make our own decisions and refuse to listen to the voice of God, we find ourselves in trouble. The Bible says in Psalm 37:5-6 (NIV), *"Commit your way to the Lord; trust in him and he will do this: He will make your righteous reward shine like the dawn, your vindication like the noonday sun."* So, although you can't see your own full potential or the future, God knows exactly where He wants to place your feet in times of confusion, defeat, pain, struggle, near death experiences, hurt, rejection, childhood memories, bullying, physical, domestic, and emotional abuse, physical battles, and spiritual battles. Through the good and the bad, He knows.

In all honesty, I had no idea I could even write a book, but it's through the power and words of my testimony and, most importantly, the Holy Spirit that I am able to. Now I realize that God allows each and every one of His children to have a testimony, so that through Him we can help someone else. This was how it all started with me. From the womb, God called me and then chose me. He knew my name before I knew my name. He knew my thoughts, my ways, my secrets, the rejection, the pain, the tears, the stress, and what would bring joy to my heart and His. He saw my smile after every obstacle, and now He can see me tell the story of His saving grace on my life, a life that did not deserve it. He sent His one and only Son, Jesus Christ, to die for each and every single thing enclosed in this book. As a matter of fact, when you think about it, we really don't have a say in the matter at birth, because we are not able to make any decisions at that stage in our life.

What I am trying to say is that my life

was ordained, even before I was born, and regardless of what should have taken place, life or death, God is the one who had the final say in my birthing process and whatever else that was to come. Even though I came out with under-developed organs, being only one pound, suffering with breathing complications, and having to be fed through tubes, God still had an ordained plan for my life, because He knew what He would have me to do on His behalf within his godly Kingdom. The same goes for you reading this book. You may not have the same testimony as me or someone else, but the moral of the story is that God is the author and finisher of our faith, according to Hebrews 12:2. Sometimes there are things in our lives that we have absolutely no control over, like our birthing process and how we look and come into this world. We just have to know that God is the master who is in control. For me, this was part of my life that I had no control over, which meant that all that I was about to go through and express in this book was already written and ordained by God. This chapter of my life, even though I was too small to even comprehend it all, would later be the reason Romans 8:28 would apply to my life. Why? Because this chapter, this stage, this birthing process, this part of my story was ordained by God. *This battle was not mine*.

CHAPTER 2

Bullying Almost Buried Me

I used to walk away crying from every situation that involved bullying, because I was always a victim of it. Bullying can be defined as a person or influence that harms or intimidates those who are weaker. Those who have experienced bullying know that it is never a good feeling. As a matter of fact, bullying can eventually affect how people view themselves. Bullying is an unpleasant feeling that many people have either had to endure or are currently enduring, secretly. When bullying is endured secretly it causes us to think of ourselves in a negative light. Bullying, believe it or not, affects the way we view ourselves, and instead of being confident in our atmosphere, the atmosphere becomes the giant. When the atmosphere becomes the giant, the person fears what is to come from the mouths of those in that atmosphere, and the victim of bullying starts living their life in fear of what others might say and do. The Bible helped me understand that Luke 6:31 says, *"Do to others as you would like them to do to you."* I did not know what that verse really meant until I realized how much the people who bullied me did not care about putting me down or hurting me or my feelings. So, yes, this answers the question that is probably floating around in your mind, "Has Janice experienced bullying?" The answer to that question is yes! With great strength, I am able to express how I felt and how I was able to overcome the infliction of bullying and the pain of it all.

    I can recall, very clearly, the moments when I experienced bullying at its lowest form and at its highest extreme. Now, in no way is this a pity party creatively written by me to draw you in to feel sorry for me. Absolutely not, for I have always been an overcomer with God on my side. This is just my story about what I had to endure, and maybe you know someone is being bullied, or maybe you yourself might be enduring bullying, secretly. The moral of this is that everyone has their own burdens that they may carry in a bag over their shoulders. Now, the Bible says in Psalm 55:22 (NLT), *"Give your burdens to the LORD, and he will take care of you. He will not permit the godly to slip and fall,"* and it means just that. You see, once you're in the Kingdom and you have accepted the Lord as your Saviour and the source of everything in your life, He willingly carries your burdens, your issues, your pains, and the things that you cannot bear. He wants us to depend solely upon Him to help us get through the toughest times in our lives. During the time of my constant bullying, I would find myself crying out to God, asking Him, "Why? Why do I have to be the one to endure all of this every day of my life, with no one running to my rescue, except for my sister every now and then?"

Being bullied became a lifestyle for me that I had to live day-in and day-out. From the age of eight, from elementary school all the way up to college, I hung my head in shame because I started to believe all the things that were being said about me. Not many people knew that my grades suffered greatly because of this bullying. My parents believed it was because I didn't want to focus in school. But how could I, when all of my thoughts were centered on what the other person was thinking of me, wondering all the time if someone would say something negative about my appearance or about my inability to read or write properly?

When someone is a victim of bullying, that person is usually the type that folds up and becomes very shy when in an environment full of people. You never get to really be yourself because the focus is always on the 'what if's.' This was what I had to go through. Only God knows why I had to endure this time in my life. But I do recall Romans 8:28 that says, *"And we know that God causes everything to work together for the good of those who love God and are called according to his purpose for them."* As I said in the previous chapter, I did not see my purpose, but this season was all a part of God's plan for my life. I had to go through it in order for you to have a story to read and be uplifted by. As I endured each comment made towards me, I would never let anyone see me cry, because in this society tears are considered to be a sign of weakness. But somewhere inside my heart I knew there was an unseen eye that saw every tear that fell from my eyes and ran down my cheeks. Nevertheless, I didn't always feel that help was on the way when I was going through such difficult times. That is where my faith would put things into perspective.

From a very young age, I would always ask God how come I had to endure such things while others would walk free; or how come those who mistreated me would not be punished for their actions towards me. But I can recall a scripture that speaks to situations like these. To those who are either going through bullying or has gone through it, the Bible says in Deuteronomy 32:35, *"Vengeance is Mine, and retribution, in due time their foot will slip; for the day of their disaster is at hand, and their doom hurries to meet them."* This scripture was one of the scriptures that helped me get through every moment of being bullied and every other situation that I had to go through, both openly and secretly.

    For me, bullying is one of those things that was not really talked about growing up. So, although it happened to me, the only time anyone knew that I was being bullied was when I could no longer bear the pain of being called names. Bullying, for me, happened absolutely everywhere and anywhere, but I can recall that it increased when I got to middle school and high school. Imagine being called 'eight-ball,' 'ET,' 'hammer head,' 'big baldhead,' 'bang head, 'big head girl,' 'mongoose,' and 'canine head.' These names were always called out to me in open settings by perfect strangers and even by those who called me friend. Now, you may be wondering how I felt during this time. Well, it truly messed with my thoughts about myself. It left me feeling as though I was ugly and like I would never ever be beautiful in anyone's sight. It eroded the confidence that I had inside of me, the little that was left. During this time, I felt like I was good for nothing. I felt the pain of being everyone's eye sore. I wondered to myself if God really loved me. I mean, how could God love me if He was allowing all of these hurtful things to happen to me? I couldn't understand how human beings could make fun of God's creation every waking day. It happened when I played basketball on school teams, even when I was in college. Imagine getting the ball passed to you and hearing the entire gym filled with fans scream, "Hammer head will make it!" or "Look at her forehead, it's so huge!" Keep in mind that this would happen at home games and away games, so I could not get away from it. It affected my game, because the entire gym had a say in how I looked, and it made me feel so low about myself. My coach at the time didn't know that my game was being affected because of the crowd making fun of me. Being one of the starters on my high school team, I knew that my coach needed me, yet as a victim of bullying I felt as though my atmosphere was a giant to me. I was intimidated by my atmosphere, broken inside yet still moving, mentally tormented but still thinking of how to love my enemies. I couldn't have felt any smaller.

I can remember a moment in time when I had to wait on a bus to get home. But before I get into that experience, let me explain that it was by choice that my friends were so selected, based on how I treated others, and that was with love. So, the popular people in school, well at least the ones I thought were popular, were the ones who were rude and obnoxious, who didn't care about anyone's feelings. These were the ones who picked on me. Taking the bus was my main transportation to get to and from school at the time, so I would wait on the city transit, the TTC. While waiting, my encounters would go something like this: "Hey, look, there is that big-headed girl again, bet she can think outside her head."

Believe it or not, one day I got angry and lashed out at the young man who said this to me. But, of course, a group of his friends surrounded me and, all alone waiting on the bus, fear grew inside of me. There was no help, no one to call on, no one. As they made a circle round about me, the young man picked up a slightly filled Orange Crush soda can off the ground and threw it at me.

He said, "This is what you get for acting up."

The soda got all over my face and hair. As I cried and screamed, I looked up and saw the bus in the distance. Everyone that surrounded me ran off. The bus came, and I got on.

The bus driver looked at me and asked me if I was okay as I wiped the sticky pop from my face.

I said, "Yes, I will be fine."

Truthfully, I was not okay. But something inside me allowed me to brush it off and keep going. I am sure you must be saying, "What? Janice, you did not tell your parents or anyone?" Well, the answer to that is no. I always had an inner-strength, and even though I would cry, and although I would hurt and go through feelings of depression, I knew that peace would find me in the morning. There is a scripture that reminds me of this time in my life, and it is located in Psalms 30:5—*"For his anger lasts only a moment, but his favor lasts a lifetime! Weeping may last through the night, but joy comes with the morning."* So before, and even after, knowing Christ I believe that God was with me and that He gave me the strength to be a contender and to approach life without fear.

Fear has a way of crippling and preventing you from moving forward in the things that God has gifted you to do. It says in 2 Timothy 1:7, *"For God has not given us a spirit of fear and timidity, but of power, love, and self-discipline."* This was the case with me. This season of bullying was truly hard to get through, but regardless of how painful it was being called names and having things thrown at me, deep down inside I knew that God had a reason, and although I could not see the reason or understand everything, He knew what He was doing.

Now, someone might ask the question, "Janice, do you experience the name-calling every now and then?" The answer is yes, most definitely. But now that I am mature enough to handle the situation, when I hear the name-calling I am able to let the individual know that that is not nice to say, and I do let them know that I would not expect that from them.

However, in most circumstances, I let the Lord handle the words that come from the heart of man. The Bible tells us that the Lord created each person in his own image (Genesis 1:27). If I were to give you some helpful advice, it would be that whenever someone makes fun of you in public, or if someone bullies you for absolutely no reason, keep this scripture in the back of your mind, if you can. Know that they are insulting God's handiwork—you. Whenever I hear or see someone getting bullied or made fun of, I can easily stick up for that person and stand in the gap to correct the person doing the bullying.

In spite of what came my way during that season, I knew that God was with me, because my experiences during my season of bullying should have made me lose my mind completely. The bullying should have rightfully buried me. But now when I look back and I think things over, God had a reason for me to go through this season of outward ridicule. Regardless of whether it was large or small, at the end of the day I can once again say that *this battle was not mine*.

CHAPTER 3

Reflecting on My Rejection

It is one thing to have a testimony, but it is another thing to reflect on your testimony and the things that God allowed you to go through and to get through. Most times, we go through things and we tend to hide it because, let's face it, not everyone can handle your testimony. Why? Because within your testimony there are things like neglect, rejection, suffering, pain, sadness, abuse, molestation, and the list could go on. Each of those things carries weight. It carries weight because it was what you had to go through in order to become who God wanted you to be. Yet, regardless of the things that take place in your life, whether you are a believer or not, God still has a plan for your life. Without a shadow of doubt, I know that many people have faced at least one of the things I mentioned above. It could be the stress from working at a particular job, or negative encounters with family members, or a friend who you thought had your best interest at heart but it happened to be the opposite. Or maybe at some point you experienced something that caused you to fold up and caused you to change your perspective on life, and it has somehow forced you to grow, depending on the situation. In this chapter, I would like to touch on the topic of rejection and what rejection can do to an individual if it is not dealt with.

First of all, in order to understand the things that we go through, it is important to study the root of the problem. It is important to know what we are going through, and especially what it means. The word *rejection* can be defined as "a refusal to accept, approve, or support something; or a refusal to show someone the love or kindness that they need or expect."[3] These two definitions for the word rejection can relate to two different situations that we face in our daily lives. The first definition can relate to the corporate life that we live, or our outside relationships, which includes school, work, church, or just going about our daily lives amongst complete strangers. The second definition can relate to our immediate

---

3 *http://www.macmillandictionary.com/dictionary/british/rejection*

families, our spouses and those closest to us or those in our inner circle. Now that you have an idea of what the word rejection means, I am sure you have experienced it at least once in your life.

The fear of rejection, believe it or not, prevents many people from forming close relationships with others. This is because victims of rejection begin to feel that they are not worthy of anyone's time, they feel that they're a bother, and they compare their situations to those who resemble their rejecter. This is due to being rejected numerous times. Rejection inflicts us with fear the minute we refuse to confront the fear of rejection. This goes hand in hand with the previous chapter where I touched on the effects that bullying had on me.

Rejection can damage a person, mentally and emotionally, because we tend to feel and think things first before dissecting what is worth fighting for and what is not. Throughout my life, I've realized that rejection happens to everyone. Some of the lies that we sometimes tell ourselves secretly are "I never feel rejected," or "I do feel rejected, but it doesn't affect or bother me," but rejection comes in many different ways and, yes, rejection does hurt and does affect the victim. So anyone who says that rejection does not affect them, tell them to truly reflect on their rejection while looking in the mirror.

Now that I have explained why it is so important to know what we go through and why we go through it, I would like to testify in this chapter, once more. Rejection was a part of my life that I seemed to always experience ever since I was a little girl. The rejection I experienced caused me to feel like I had a red X marked on me, as though I was a target from the very beginning. Throughout this time, rejection caused me to shed many tears and ask God why He would allow all of this to happen. I submitted and committed my life to Jesus at the age of eleven and, technically, this warranted me and anyone who is a follower of Jesus Christ to feel what Jesus had to feel. The Bible lets us know that when Jesus was here on Earth, He experienced rejection that was not ordinary. Jesus also tells us that those who make the choice to follow Him will suffer for His name's sake. This means that because we are followers of Christ, we will experience hardships, but these hardships help us to develop a dependency on God rather than man. While going through our own individual trials and issues, we develop endurance, and through endurance strength, and with strength a healthy character that reflects Him.

My rejection started in elementary school, but I did not realize it at that time, being so young. But now when I reflect and think things over and testify about what I had to endure, I can vividly remember when I would desire to take part in the extra-curricular activities the school offered but would never qualify. The elementary school that I went to had school plays, plays such as *The Wizard of Oz* and *Snow White*. I remember trying out to sing the lead role for one of these plays, but I was not selected. They placed me in the choir every single year, something I just didn't want to do, but I ended up doing it anyway. Being rejected every year caused me to believe that my singing ability was not what they were looking for, but through that I kept moving forward. And for those who know me, you know that I love to sing but never believed in my singing ability due to the constant rejection from people. Every time I went to the next grade level, I realized a pattern—many of the things that teachers and principals felt I could not do, I could do. Things like reading and writing. They expressed that I was not up to standard like everyone else in the class, which meant that I had to sit in a class with those who had difficulty reading and writing—special education classes. It was like the school tried to make me believe that I was incapable of reading and writing. Throughout this time, I remember always trying to hide in my actual class so I wouldn't have to join the special education class, only to hear my name called to head out to that class. This was a form of rejection, because I felt like I was not given a chance to prove them wrong, and every time I questioned it, I was turned down. But yet again, I continued on without allowing it to get me down, especially being so young.

My life was filled with rejection, but I did not take the time to foster the importance of the rejection. As I got older, I realized that my rejection from jobs, school, ministry, and many other areas in life would not disappear. Now that I am older and way more mature, I understand why I had to endure the rejections, because rejections, knowingly or unknowingly, are meant to build us up as followers of Jesus Christ. It wasn't until I experienced every rejection in my life that I realized that God was pruning me to stand firmly under pressure and to understand that He is in control of every one of my steps. So, if you are facing rejection from family, friends, the church, school, or on the job, usually it means that God is trying to birth something inside of you, or He is trying to protect you from the filthy hands of the enemy. My encouraging word to you, if you are facing rejection, is to allow God to continue to do His ordained work inside of you. Don't view the rejection or the trying times around the rejection as God punishing you or neglecting you, because it can sometimes seem like that. But view the rejection as a pruning process, a time for character building and birthing of the next level that He has for your life.

Another form of rejection that I faced was rejection from the opposite sex. Yes, my ability to form and keep intimate relationships, or what we call dating, was truly a task for me. Why? Because, truth be told, anyone who has suffered rejection, unless they are healed or delivered from it, has a hard time forming relationships with others. The level of trust varies when someone gets involved with the opposite sex. It varies because the underlying problem, or the root of the problem, has not been dealt with—the feelings of rejection. So, every time the opportunity presented itself to date or be with someone, I would say, "Yes," but my mind and heart were far off. I was not fully devoted to it. You know that scripture in Proverbs 4:23 that says, *"Guard your heart above all else, for it determines the course of your life"*? That was one of the scriptures I held on to in every relationship, but I was not using it correctly, in the biblical sense, because deep down I knew that I was only filling voids on top of not being delivered from my own past hurts and rejections. That is why it is so important to get healed and delivered from rejection and anything that hurts you. Being involved with someone always had me feeling afraid that the person would reject me and the love I offered from my heart. And the moment the person realized this in me, he would pack up everything and leave with the famous line, "We just don't mesh, or click, anymore." Sometimes they would just walk away from me without conversation or reason.

Every time I was in a relationship, I realized

that God wanted to fix this issue of rejection and not wanting to take a chance at building healthy relationships. Now, anyone who is in a relationship knows that it's either you're in it one hundred percent or not at all. My rejection caused me to be selective in the things that I did and shared with my significant other at the time, and this came from an unsettled place within me. The moral of this rejection, where relationships were concerned, was that God wanted me to know that as I matured I needed to deal with my rejection and my feelings. So, what needed to be done was for me to seek God and let Him know that rejection was affecting my daily life with others and causing me to doubt healthy relationships, which prevented me from moving forward. With that being said, I had to submit my rejection to him. I had to learn why I was going through this issue. It was only through submitting and resubmitting every moment of my rejection to Him that I would be available to be used properly for His glory. Just a word of advice, no one can force you to be delivered, you have to want it; there has to be a call inside of you that you want to answer. I wanted to answer this call because I realized that I couldn't want to be positive or want to lead and bleed at the same time. So, once I came to that stage of answering the call of God inside of me, He immediately began to perform both surgery and healing at the same time. And guess what? It was a very painful process. It was then that I realized that the Lord had a plan, and His plan was to repair me so I could live free from my rejection and every baggage that came with it. But if I did not listen to the still inner-voice speaking to me, I probably would have ignored the operation God wanted to do. That was when I realized that this battle of rejection was just not mine. *The battle was just not mine*, yet again.

CHAPTER 4

The Wilderness Experience

God always knows what He is going to do, when He is going to do it, why He is going to do it, where He is going to do it, and how He is going to do it, without needing anyone's permission to do it. Yet, the majority of the time we, as humans, want to take matters into our own hands and be the god in our own lives, thinking we can accomplish what we want, when we want, and how we want. We feel a sense of accomplishment whenever we achieve something. Why? Well, our flesh is always looking for some type of satisfaction. The Bible says in Matthew 26:41, *"Watch and pray so that you will not fall into temptation. The spirit is willing, but the flesh is weak."* There are times when God wants us to go through a particular situation to let us gain wisdom, knowledge, understanding, and even endurance. Many times, God will allow us to go through these seasons alone. I call these particular experiences "the wilderness experience." I call it the wilderness experience because there was a time in the Bible when God was trying to deliver His chosen people. God's plan was to give His chosen people the Promised Land, but they refused what God was trying to teach them, which was to trust Him in the midst of their situation. The wilderness experience can be defined as a lonely place where God desires to get our attention for a specific reason. The majority of the time, He does this to speak through us and to us about something specific. Unfortunately, sometimes while He is trying to get our attention, we are occupied by our own desires, which can then become a distraction. It is during this time that God is trying to take us to the next destination on the roadmap He has for our lives.

My wilderness experience was exactly what it sounds like. There were quite a few moments when I would experience feeling alone, not only that, but I would feel as though God had forgotten me. I realize that there were many times in my life when I was stubborn to the voice of the Lord. For example, when the Lord called for me to do a certain thing and to do it without fear, I would either shy away from it or run away from the entire situation.

But then I realized that the Lord caused me to have to come to Him and surrender all my issues, my ways, my habits, my thoughts, my pride, and everything that was standing in the way of Him doing a new thing in my life. I can clearly recall a time when God was just quiet on a few things that were happening in my life. During this time, I began to ask Him "Why?" but it felt like He was far away, and I just could not understand. Yes, I fasted from everything that caused the distractions and the things that prevented me from hearing His voice, yet still nothing. Yes, I even stayed up late, burning the midnight oil, praying, and seeking the face of God, yet still no communication from Him. This was truly a wilderness experience. Imagine wanting to hear from God. As a matter of fact, imagine always hearing from Him, always hearkening to His voice, knowing full well that when you listened to Him victory was made yours. Now imagine experiencing not one piece of communication from your best friend—that's exactly what God is to me, my best friend, so not hearing from Him caused me to wonder what to do. My passion to seek Him during this time began to fall off, and at times pick up, almost like a teeter totter in a park. It was up and down, and it almost felt like there was going to be no return.

This wilderness experience became everything to me, because I realized that everything under the sun came to find me as a result of me opening the door to it. The Bible tells us in 1 Peter 5:8, *"Stay alert! Watch out for your great enemy, the devil. He prowls around like a roaring lion, looking for someone to devour."* During this quiet and silent time, I realized that I left the doors of my soul open for the enemy to creep in. That is what the enemy is looking for, a tiny crack or opening. The enemy waits at open doors, not closed ones. With that being said, the enemy waits for the perfect opportunity to entice us with the things that we love and take delight in. Not only that, but the devil also tries us with the things that we struggle with.

During this wilderness experience, it was like I was walking down a road of loneliness, filled with fear of the unknown. My life on this road appeared to be very difficult, and I just had no idea why. But through this experience, I realized that the wilderness resembles exactly what the word means. The term *wilderness* can be defined as "a neglected or abandoned area; uncultivated, uninhabited and inhospitable area or region."[4] Now, you may be asking how a definition like this describes my own wilderness experience. Well, I neglected myself and ended up walking down a road that was only filled with empty promises. I placed myself in undeserving situations, craved sin instead of who God had called me to be in Him and, at some point, I was angry

---

4 https://en.oxforddictionaries.com/definition/us/wilderness

and broken inside because nothing was going right. This then led me to become very quiet and nonchalant towards anything and anyone who came in my path while I walked through this wilderness experience.

While walking through this wilderness, I got bitten, chased, and tormented in my thoughts, not physically but mentally. As I walked on this road, I realized that I neglected my immediate family. I mistreated them, turned a deaf ear to them, felt like I was the one who was always right and they never were, kept thinking and saying that they didn't love me, and I began to isolate myself, began to believe this lie the devil was feeding me. Not only that, but I decided that I was going to have my own way with my life, and nothing and no one could stand in the way of that. While in this wilderness experience, I recall roaming and looking for the uttermost fulfillment with man; that didn't really fill me up but left me feeling empty and broken all over again.

This wilderness experience was probably God trying to get my attention to seek Him and to turn from my wicked ways, because He was calling me. After all, He says, *"If my people who are called by my name will humble themselves pray and seek my face and turn from their wicked ways, I will hear from heaven and will forgive their sins and restore their land"* (2 Chronicles 7:14). This scripture could refer to me because I would always hear a prophetic word from those that God would send my way. The prophetic word was that I was called and chosen for the Lord's work, but I did not believe it nor did I understand the reason why I was chosen. It also refers to the land that I was walking upon, the area in which I decided to place my feet.

This wilderness experience was not holy; it did not reflect Christ, and I knew in my heart that it wasn't of God. With that being said, I believe that God desired for me to go through it to help another soul. It caused me to look inwardly at my secret sins, thinking He would not see me, but that was far from the truth, because the Lord sees all and He is a rewarder of the good things that we do. And, yes, I can truly say that I did not always walk in the Spirit according to the scriptures. The Holy Word of God tells us in Galatians 5:16-18, *"So I say, walk by the Spirit, and you will not gratify the desires of the flesh. For the flesh desires what is contrary to the Spirit and the Spirit what is contrary to the flesh. They are in conflict with each other, so that you are not to do whatever you want. But if you are led by the Spirit, you are not under the law."*

Due to this wilderness experience that I probably caused on myself without knowing, I was not consistent. Yet, for some reason, God had a plan in mind and a story behind the lessons. This experience surely caused me to relive a few stories, quite a few times. And usually when you have to go through the same lesson two or three times, it means you have not yet grasped the concept in order to pass. It's just like failing a math class a couple of times, it just means you have not yet grasped the material or the lesson. This experience helped me to realize that although I felt alone, although I thought God was nowhere to be found, and although I wanted to do everything my own way, God was watching me. There is a song that says, "He looked beyond my faults and saw my needs." As I went through this experience, I realized that when I finally made the decision to look to God and turn over these things that were happening to me in the wilderness, I was able to experience true liberty and freedom to do exploits in Him. When I began to give up my own ways—my pride, my anger, my bitterness—that I thought I did not have, the minute I threw in the towel on settling for second best where relationships with the opposite sex were concerned, when I truly looked fear and defeat in the face and said, "God is and will be my rock and fortress," when I truly said, "I surrender this wilderness to you and I will trust you, Lord, comes what may," I was able to see a light at the end of the road.

That light got closer and closer to me as I began to be submissive to the Lord and the call He distinctly had on my life. When I decided to give it all up—every obstacle I enjoyed running into—that was when the light began to shine. The minute I got to the end of the wilderness experience for that season, God began to reveal to me the gifts He placed inside of me and that my life had a purpose. His light began to shine upon my feet; He truly became a lamp unto my feet, as His Word says. God began to remove the layers and masks that I was wearing that only I knew of. His light became a home inside of my heart, soul, and mind. His will began to take control of my life. I realized that, as I began to trust Him, He was looking out for me. His hand was truly upon my life. I did not fully know my own next step, but I knew this experience had shaped me and molded me into a new creation. The Bible declares that those who are in Christ are made a new creation (2 Corinthians 5:17).

As I became this new creation, I began to act like Him and I began to indulge in His Word to find out what He was trying to do in me. To be transparent, I would kind of stress a little, because I wanted to make sure I was in the perfect will of God and not outside of it. So I started to take my walk seriously, knowing full well that I was not perfect; as a matter of fact, none of us is perfect. With that being said, I realized that I still needed to trust Him more, but it was better to be on the right path than to walk on a lonely one, fighting my own battles without the Lord. As the Lord began to guide me, He began to reveal to me why I had to go through this lonely experience, although He was right there waiting for me.

This chapter is called The Wilderness Experience because just as it was in the Bible when the Children of Israel were going in circles, so it was with me. I was going in circles, doing the same thing over and over, only to realize that my will was not God's will. I say all of this to say to the precious soul reading this chapter of my book that if you are experiencing a lonely season, if you feel like you need the things of this world to satisfy you, or feel like you know what is best for you, I encourage you to take a leap of faith and find out who God is, if you don't know Him already. If you do know Him and you are simply struggling with your own fleshy desires, just like me, and you feel it is a stronghold of some sort, seek assistance from a trustworthy brother or sister within the church or a true minister of the gospel who demonstrates the fruits of the Spirit. Galatians 5:22-23 will help you know who to trust with your wilderness experience as it pertains to seeking help. Everyone needs someone to help them through their wilderness experience. I purposely left out the names of the people who ran to my rescue in order to prove to you that the Lord orchestrates all things, and He does speak through people. This is one way to know that He is speaking to you and through you, because if it was not for the faithful few who held my hand along the way, I probably wouldn't be in this position to tell this story. This chapter of my life proved to me that *the battle was not mine*, yet again, and I am glad it wasn't.

CHAPTER 5

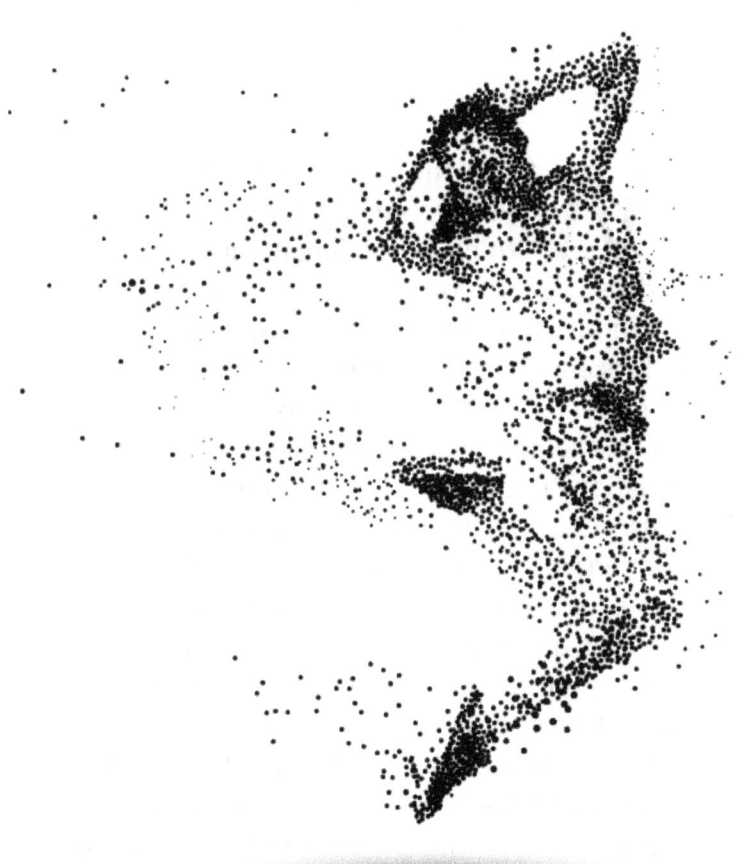

Broken to Peace

When the word *broken* is used, it usually means that a particular thing is not functioning properly and is out of order. When some*thing* is broken it is no different than when some*one* is broken. The only difference between the some*thing* and the some*one* is the reason for the brokenness. Many times we go through situations not able to pinpoint the things that cause us to be broken. The reason why that happens is that we don't take a look at the things we invite or allow into our lives until we end up in a situation that causes us to feel broken and to look for peace. It is natural to feel broken when our hearts are broken, when someone betrays our trust and love, when someone tells lies on us, or when we are deceived or manipulated without seeing it before it happens. Brokenness can cause you to experience a sense of vulnerability because of what was meant to destroy you. Sometimes you will have those around you give you a look that says, "What is going on with this woman or man?" And if you're not careful, sometimes the world and people you thought would look out for you can end up dropping you during your time of brokenness. As a matter of fact, the world, believe it or not, has a tendency to throw broken things into the garbage. Not just broken things, but also things despised are tossed into the garbage or, in this case, cast away, or seen as outcasts.

Often, we see brokenness as being a sign of weakness, but in actuality it is intended to humble us before the Lord and make us stronger through Him. When we reach our breaking point in a particular situation, relationship, or personal circumstance, as believers in Jesus Christ, it causes us to give birth to a deep sincerity to seek the Lord. Believe it or not, our brokenness works in our favour. Psalm 34:18 says, *"The Lord is close to the brokenhearted; he rescues those whose spirits are crushed."* This verse helps us know that our brokenness is not overlooked; it is actually used for His glory. To the world, brokenness is seen as something that should be thrown away. To God, brokenness is seen as His way of reshaping and remaking us. When we do not allow the Lord to break us, mold us, and make us through circumstances and situations that we sometimes put ourselves in, we are telling Him that we don't need Him. If we portray that we do not need Him, our process becomes difficult, and the situation or issue that is supposed to make us stronger ends up holding us back from the process that the Lord is trying to perfect in us. The Lord knows that we have many things inside of us that need to be broken, such as pride, jealousy, stubbornness, self-will, arroganance, sinful habits and behaviours, just to name a few. When the Lord breaks the things that hinder us, it is His way of letting us know that His desire is for us to be fully surrendered to His will.

In most cases, coming to a place of brokenness is pretty much the only way to find peace. Many people, all across the world, think being broken is a sign of weakness. Although society tells us that anything broken deserves to be put in the garbage bin, Jesus does not throw us away or leave us alone when we appear happy on the outside but are broken on the inside. God sees our brokenness as a tool for Him to use for His glory.

Before writing this book, I personally took on the word broken and took society's meaning of the word. As I began to let the word sink deeply into my spirit, the Lord began to reveal to me the depth of this word. In the natural sense, the word means exactly what it says. In the spiritual, God sees it as the opposite. When He looks at us, His creation, it means repairable, moldable, and a new creation.

Like I said before, I viewed brokenness through the world's interpretation—irreparable and absolutely unfixable. This brings me to the secret brokenness that I experienced. As I began to have numerous encounters with the Lord, He began to reveal to me that I had to be broken on the inside in order for Him to use me as one of His end-time tools for my generation and those He had attached to me. My brokenness came from an inner-part of me. Things like fear, defeat, disbelief, anger, pain, bitterness, and doubt were just some of the things I was dealing with silently throughout the years. I did not have control over them; as a matter of fact, I did not allow God to take control of these areas that caused me to feel broken. The only way to honestly break free from these areas was to repent to God for not allowing Him to have His way within me. So, yes, I had to repent to the Lord Jesus, and the bitterness, the lack of faith through disbelief, the anger, the pain, the doubt, and everything that became a stumbling block or a hindrance to the Lord doing His work in me had to be submitted to Him. These things would happen because I allowed them to happen. The Bible says in Matthew 7:7, *"Ask and it will be given to you; seek and you will find; knock and the door will be opened to you."* This scripture lets me know that anything we ask of the Lord, if it is in His will, He will grant it to us. However, on the opposite side of this, the devil also waits at open doors, not closed ones. So, with that being said, even though we are asking the Lord to do something on our behalf, whether that means to come into our heart or to help us with a situation, always remember that the devil—the enemy, the ruler of darkness—is always lying in wait to distract us. This was the case with my brokenness. I did not have peace in the midst of all these storms.

Brokenness always stems from an underlying problem or situation that is taking place within us. It is usually a deeply rooted thing that we hang on to that causes us to react the way we do. But we also have a choice in whether we want deliverance from brokenness. It is when we are delivered by the Lord that we are truly delivered. It is then that we can honestly say, "Yes, I have been delivered!"

My experience with brokenness during certain situations was to teach me a lesson. Now, although certain experiences would hurt, I knew that God was putting my feet on a pathway towards peace. But it was totally up to me to want deliverance from myself and from putting myself in situations that would result in me feeling broken. Many of my secret issues caused me to notice my brokenness, the brokenness God wanted me to experience so that I could experience His peace. This brings me to the fruit I've been mentioning in this chapter—peace.

Peace is being free from disturbance, it is tranquility and calmness. This peace that I speak of is the peace you encounter after you've been broken down by the Lord. This is when everything around you has come to a halt and things are beyond your control. This peace comes to you when you have willfully surrendered every broken situation to Jesus Christ. The presence of peace only came to my life when I willfully gave over my disobedient ways to Christ and traded them in for His obedience. Although my life resembled that of a peacemaker, within my heart the peace of God was absent. This was a peace that only Jesus Christ could give me. When you think about it, it does not make sense to always be the peacemaker yet lack your own personal peace, the one that the Bible says we should have (Colossians 3:15). It is possible to have spiritual fruits that have not yet fully grown. My spiritual tree, for example, had branches that needed to be pruned, so that each fruit of the Spirit could grow and produce good fruit. If you ever look at a tree that needs to be pruned, branches are usually growing all over the place. However, pruning the tree helps to stimulate the growth of the tree. So, where there are dead branches or extremely long branches, they must be cut down to improve the growth of the tree. This principle can also be applied to the spiritual fruits we bear within us as children of God.

My fruit of peace did not taste good to me, and I had to realize this through my brokenness. Every now and then, it is important, as believers in Jesus Christ, to look within ourselves to see if our spiritual fruits are growing healthily. In order to have peace within ourselves, God wants us to submit our cares to Him. He truly cares about everything we think He may not care about. For it is during those times when we think He does not care that He wants to make His peace available to us. You see, when you have peace, the peace that passes all understanding, virtuous qualities develop within you, like unity, harmony, forgiveness, and a perfect understanding and attitude. Whether you're a woman or man, inner-peace allows you to demonstrate grace towards others. The minute we are without inner-peace, sin gains entry into our lives, and we begin to feel depressed, stressed, angry, worried, and may even question or lash out on God or those closest to us.

Yes, when we lack peace, all sorts of things begin to happen within us that cause us to act out of ourselves. The reason we act out of ourselves is that without peace, we suffer from an internal war. For me, my peace had to come from completely being honest with the

Lord and, most importantly, being honest with myself and letting Jesus take full control of my heart and life. The Bible says in Philippians 4:7, *"And the peace of God, which surpasses all understanding, will guard your hearts and your minds in Christ Jesus."* This was the only peace that could prevent me from feeling broken and undone within. So my decision was to seek the Lord Jesus for peace. As I began to seek Him for peace, He surely began to reveal Himself to me. He let me know that in order to have peace I had to release myself from wanting control over everything in my heart and in my life. In return, having His peace would help me treat others with His grace.

Peace is very important for the believer in Christ, because when you're broken, it interferes with both the true ministry that God wants to do within you and what you have to give to others. So before finding peace, you must first understand the root of your brokenness, seek forgiveness from God, and ask Him to enter into your heart to give you the peace that passes all understanding. Believe it or not, it's easy for those around you to know if you demonstrate this fruit of the Spirit called peace; it will show on your countenance. My brokenness at times didn't really show on the outside, but when I had to deal with others it protruded on the surface, and it was during these times that God began to show me things about myself that needed to change. The fruit of peace was not ripening within me or, in this case, maturing the way God wanted it to, because I was so in control of how I distributed peace to others. This proved to me that I was broken inside, and the roots of peace looked like brokenness rather than the peace that passes all understanding. As the Lord began to reveal all of this to me, He proved to me that the devil needs the Lord's permission to make certain things happen to us. In my case, my brokenness was attached to many of my freewill intentions due to my stubborn mentality. There is a saying that my mother always used to remind me of whenever someone did negative things to me, she said, "Sometimes you have to learn the hard way."

Of course, my brokenness taught me a lesson, it taught me that I needed to fully rely on God for all things, and to repent to the Lord for not allowing Him to take full control over my emotions and break me down. His breaking me was to build me. The only time I give advice is when I experience a situation that I know God can use to help others; the brokenness that I endured and inflicted upon myself is a prime example. The advice that I would so gladly give to a young man or woman is if you're experiencing brokenness internally due to excess baggage, the only thing that you can do is be true to yourself, repent, and begin to give it over to Jesus. You will see that the Lord is able to take your feelings of brokenness away, and He will replace them with His peace, the peace that passes all understanding. It wasn't until I became honest with myself about my brokenness—the hurt, the pain, the secret of wanting to forgive myself and others, the anger, the self-will, the self-neglect—that I received a peace that kept me smiling. Truly, I had to sit and think, and a still voice spoke to me and clearly said that *this battle was not mine*.

CHAPTER 6

The Revolving Door:
Matters of the Heart

Life can be compared to many things. One minute we're up, the next minute we're down, but at the end of the day things happen *for* us and not *to* us. Life can sometimes be seen as a revolving door filled with many different life experiences, whether good or bad. In this chapter, I want you to envision a revolving door. A revolving door is a door that allows large numbers of people to pass in and out. Revolving doors often consist of four doors, each door is called a wing or leaf, and they spread an equal distance from each other around a centre shaft. A revolving door tends to change personnel on a frequent basis. Revolving doors require you to keep your feet moving in order to get through to the other side. At times it gets difficult, because with every revolving door you encounter different people focused on getting through the same system as you. Oftentimes, if someone is slowing you down in front, the door will either stall or stop, which causes you to get stuck. This is because someone slowed down the process and interfered with you getting to where you're going, which is on the other side.

A revolving door can mirror our individual lives, because the same way we invite people into our lives, or indulge in places or things, is the same way a revolving door operates. Sometimes we do not see or discern the people who might take us for granted, so we unknowingly allow people to enter or be a part of our lives without even asking God if this is His perfect will or permissive will. When this happens, we end up having some really good or bad experiences. Oftentimes, our experiences have a tendency to repeat themselves, similar to a revolving door. In other words, when one situation runs out another runs in. Yes, it is possible to relive certain situations with the same people, go to the same places, and indulge in the same activities, over and over again. This causes us to experience a revolving door pattern inside of our heart, mind, and soul.

The question you may be asking is, "What next can Janice possibly say about this revolving door example?" Well, I am glad I got your mind thinking. My life resembled a revolving door, one that constantly spun with many different faces. When I speak about the revolving door, I speak about your heart being the revolving door—conditions of the heart. So, yes, the revolving door of my heart was open to everyone and everything, both good and bad. Not only was it open, but the revolving door of my heart also malfunctioned, because I would allow my heart to get stuck on petty things that others would do, both knowingly and unknowingly. My version of forgiveness was clouded, because I felt that forgiving someone inside my heart meant just letting that situation go or moving on without speaking or dealing with that person anymore. But true forgiveness comes from God. True forgiveness is being able to confront a situation, having a sole purpose to make things right. So when the Holy Spirit convicts you to go and make things right and you ignore Him, you cause your heart to malfunction. The result is that the revolving door of your heart begins to get stuck. Unless you walk into what the Lord is asking you to do, the revolving door of your heart will not be free to love and move forward. Earlier I mentioned that it is possible for a revolving door to get stuck when someone stops moving their feet while walking through a revolving door. Well, it is no different when we stop the flow of the Holy Spirit speaking to us. When the Lord speaks to us to make things right, we should always do just that. The minute we stop the revolving door—the will of the Holy

Spirit to fix our hearts—our hearts begin to malfunction, and we then react outside of the will of God.

I beame stuck because I did not want to submit to the Holy Spirit, who was telling me to make things right with certain people. And when you become stuck because you're not doing the will of the Father, you're then caught between a rock and a hard place. In this case, not only are you stuck in the door, but you have many people inside the door with you that you probably once knew but, because of unforgiveness, they have become strangers. The reason I say "once knew" is because usually when we don't forgive others we tend to move on and alienate them. I have done this before, and I know you probably can relate. So, yes, you can become stuck and prideful, to say the least. This is because you refuse to forgive and let go for real. You become stuck inside the revolving door, so every time you push the door, it jams. When the door malfunctions, it is usually because something or someone has slowed it down. In my case, I was slowed down because as the Lord began to do a work in me to forgive others, I would sweep it under the rug of my heart. I could feel the Holy Spirit convicting me to go and make things right with the people that I knew I had issues with inside my heart. It was very tangible. But, of course, my self-will got in the way of me doing as the Lord was leading me to do. The reason why

I share this part of my testimony is solely to let you know that, as believers in Christ, we are not perfect, although the world has the perception that we should be. Our hearts are tested daily to see how much we line up with the will of God the Father as He directs us.

This experience caused me to do a heart check to make sure that my heart was not being fooled by Satan, the biggest deceiver. Once he gets a hold of a person's heart, it can wax cold towards what is just and righteous. The Bible says in Jeremiah 17:9, *"The heart is deceitful above all things, and desperately wicked; who can know it?"* No one! I repeat: no one can see the intentions of the heart. The revolving door of my heart had to be made clear of all the hidden things that were hindering me from getting to the next level that God had for my life. I felt that as long as I was nice to others that that was good enough. I didn't take the time to look deeper into what lies within my own heart. For example, if I had something against my brother or sister in the Body of Christ, with my family members, or with people in general, I would ignore forgiveness and go about my business as though things were okay, even though inside my heart the Holy Spirit would convict me. And even though it was uncomfortable, I would turn down the voice of the Lord telling me to make things right. You see, the ability to shun the very sight of forgiveness, the ability to completely walk away from someone I once knew, was very easy for me. Yet, deep down inside, I would hear the voice of God telling me that He would prefer that I ask for forgiveness and not appear as though I am without blemish.

I know for a fact that many people have, at some point in their lives, experienced unforgiveness lingering on the inside of their hearts; you know, that revolving door, that gateway to your heart that absolutely no one has the ability to see but God. Realistically, people don't have x-ray vision when it comes to seeing the heart, so this is where God and His Word come into the picture. God's Word can allow you to see into a person's heart. There is a saying that I used to always hear when I was going through this painful revolving door experience, and I am sure you've heard it, too. It states, "Forgiveness is not for the other person, forgiveness is for you." To be honest, when you look real deep into that saying, you begin to realize that this is the hard truth.

Revolving doors malfunction when something within the function of the door is corrupted. This can also apply to you and me; our hearts begin to malfunction when we operate outside of the will of God. When I truly thought about how my heart was beating and what was inside of it, I realized that it was not aligned with how God wanted it to be. Your heart reflects the real you. Think about this for a second, if the heart was not important to

God, He would not look at it first. If the heart was not important to God, He would not have used a tree to illustrate the heart change—your fruit flows from the heart. By this I mean that how you act and behave shows what kinds of fruits are being grown and how rooted and grounded you truly are in Jesus Christ. The same way you can recognize a tree by its fruits is the same way you can recognize other people by how they act in God. God was working on my heart, and continues to work on my heart, because He knows that I am not perfect and He knows that we all fall short of His glory.

With all of this being said, God wants you and me to give our hearts to Him. It will forever be a losing battle when we follow our own desires without adhering to God's voice. The Bible says in Proverbs 23:26, *"My son, give me your heart and let your eyes keep to my ways."* And then again in Matthew 5:8 it says, *"Blessed are the pure in heart, for they shall see God."* These scriptures tell us that God looks closely at the heart of man, looking at our intentions, wanting us to have a close relationship with Him and others. Through this, I knew God wanted a close relationship with me. He wanted me to build an altar in my heart to Him and Him alone. But my actions were different, because I just did not want to do it. I didn't "seek first the Kingdom" as He wanted me to. Moreover, I wanted my own way. I wanted to do my own thing, on my own time. Yet still, there I was boldly asking Him to bless me and help me get to another level in Him.

I believe that living a life of truth is very important, as it goes hand in hand with living a life of integrity. So I highly believe in telling on yourself. It is the best thing you could possibly do, especially as a believer in Jesus Christ, because, let's be truthful, people enjoy the sound of gossip whenever it concerns people in the Body of Christ. The best way to clear up any type of gossip before it hits the ears of others is to tell on yourself. Information is always relevant when it comes from the horse's mouth, so here I am. Before the Lord spoke to me about submitting my revolving door and the matters of my heart to Him, I didn't want to. The reason I didn't want to was because I was comfortable with how things were—not having to apologize for my wrong doing, not feeling as if I owed anything to anyone was the best feeling. But the feeling only lasted for a period of time; it lasted as long as I turned down the voice of God in my spirit. The truth is, there will come a point when you will get tired of running from the truth, especially if you claim or say you have the Holy Spirit living on the inside of you. This was the case with me. The end to my race came when the Lord intercepted me and arrested me because of the matters I had in my own heart.

Trust me, it was not easy at all. I felt like

it was impossible to quit something I enjoyed, especially if I was having my own way with it. However, when the Lord Jesus Christ came into my heart and started to direct my feet towards righteousness, I realized that it just wasn't as bad as I thought. If I claimed to be a disciple of Jesus Christ and I claimed to believe in Him, then I should adhere to His truth once He reveals or tells me to do something. The Bible tells us in John 8:31-32 that, *"Jesus said to the people who believed in him, 'You are truly my disciples if you remain faithful to my teachings. And you will know the truth, and the truth will set you free.'"*

The revolving door of my heart took time to function properly, because His voice needed to be clear to me concerning my life. Once I submitted my heart to the Lord, once I gave Him my all, once I listened to the Holy Spirit speaking to me, I realized that our relationship became solid. The matters of my heart—my revolving door—were no longer in my hands, because I allowed Him to gain entry into my heart. Then I realized that this battle concerning the matters of my heart, *this battle was definitely not mine.*

CHAPTER 7

The Black Sheep Experience:
The Misfit

Have you ever felt like no one understood you? Or like people accused you of having an attitude, when deep down inside you knew you didn't? Or have you ever felt as though people thought you were insensitive and rebellious, when you knew you weren't? Well, I am sorry to break this news to you, but welcome to the club. I have felt that way numerous times. When you feel like you're the outcast in society, like you stand out all the time and you just don't fit in, chances are you have a purpose. Now, let me assure you, it is never a bad thing. It just means that there is a great call upon your life that the Lord will reveal to you in due time. I call people who endure these circumstances and experiences "black sheep." They just don't fit in with the group or crowd, no matter how hard they try.

I would like you to relate to this chapter as much as possible. Can you recall a time in your life when you just did not fit into a club, church, job, or group? You just couldn't understand why you didn't fit in. You would try to look, act, and maybe even dress the part, yet still the repercussions of doing all of this just didn't amount to anything. Let me take you a little further, the characteristics of black sheep are naturally different from regular white sheep. Black sheep naturally have a genetic make-up that separates them from the rest of the flock. Black sheep are black due to a recessive trait, which naturally causes them to stand out. The black colour is undesirable and means they're unable to be dyed to any other colour. Many people viewed the black sheep as a sign of the devil, because it was somehow linked to a form of darkness. Moreover, black sheep were always looked at as having an abnormal personality.

In the previous chapter, I expressed the importance of telling on yourself, especially if others have heard or possibly lied about your character. My life at times resembled the black sheep experience. Truth be told, I was never the type of person to fit into a clique, box, group, school, choir, or sometimes even church. It became frustrating for me, because I truly wanted to be accepted in all of these things, but for some strange reason it just didn't happen. Nevertheless, rather than accepting this cold, hard truth, I forced myself to fit in, and everyone knows that it's better to break down a box than to forcibly fit into one. I felt within myself that if I fit in, it would be a lot easier to handle than to walk alone and have to endure a journey all by myself. When you think about it, I was that black sheep. In the Bible, there is a parable that speaks about the lost sheep. It explains the importance of that one sheep that Jesus went after when it wandered away.

"So Jesus told them this story: 'If a man has a hundred sheep and one of them gets lost, what will he do? Won't he leave the ninety-nine others in the wilderness and go to search for the one that is lost until he finds it? And when he has found it, he will joyfully carry it home on his shoulders. When he arrives, he will call together his friends and neighbors, saying, 'Rejoice with me because I have found my lost sheep.' In the same way, there is more joy in heaven over one lost sinner who repents and returns to God than over ninety-nine others who are righteous and haven't strayed away!'"
(Luke 15:3-7)

This passage speaks of the sheep, that if it wanders, the Lord is interested in locating it. Jesus went looking for that one black sheep that was lost. In this case, I was that one wandering black sheep that was constantly searching to fit in, constantly wanting to jump out of the will that God had for me, constantly wanting to go in the opposite direction, while following the crowd. I was always viewed as someone whom no one understood, and I am sure at times my own family could barely understand me. If you were to ask them, they would probably say that they just don't know why. Many times in families there is that one person who is just different. That person usually talks differently, works differently, and probably experiences the hardest of times. If that person is you, and you have somehow experienced being that black sheep that I speak of, you have a particular purpose.

Realistically, when you think about the reason why a sheep, or in this case a black sheep, wanders, it is because they get agitated when they're separated from a group. For me, it was the opposite. I separated myself because I just did not fit in with the crowd. I can vividly recall when I would wander far off in my mind, in my spirit, and in my soul. The reason for all this wandering was because I was seeking, seeking for something. At times, I did not know what that something was, but I knew deep down in the very depths of my soul that I was longing for an encounter with the Lord God. Truthfully, I knew that I could not find Him if I did not make a decision to seek Him. The reason I decided to share this chapter of my life in this book is because I was always considered the black sheep, at least that's what it felt like. For years, I would try to advance myself in many areas of my life but only received closed doors in my face and constantly hear, "You're no good," when initially I knew that I was everything and then some. My life reflected that of the black sheep's in many ways. I say that because I remember when I would wander far away from the Kingdom into my own personal space. In this secret place in my thoughts and in my heart, I would allow myself to indulge in searching not for the Shepherd, but for fulfillment and validation from the things of my own flesh.

My wandering became more about me and where I could go, what I could find, and how it could benefit me. So, I solely thought about myself. I appreciated my wandering moments because I can recall that anytime I was in trouble, Jesus made it His point of duty to lead me back to Him, without me knowing. The point I am trying to make is that although we may appear as black sheep, know that Jesus accepts us. The parable of the lost sheep explains to us that even when we choose to get into the mindset of the lost sheep, the Lord is the good Shepherd who is actively paying attention to the number of sheep in His sheepfold. He is not only aware of the ninety-nine sheep, but He is in tune with that one sheep that wanders off, you or me. I can relate to this black sheep experience, because there were times in my life that I just wanted to live like the world and to even dress like the world. I wanted to try everything that was exciting in the world—the latest fashion, clubs, and lounges (the safe term that people use when they say it's not a club). Again, I was wandering away from the calling and the many prophecies I had received when I was with the flock, when I was in the Kingdom. Every time I had that black sheep experience, those around me would always try to warn me; however, my inquisitive nature caused me to wander around and wander right into the hands of the enemy.

    Through this experience, I realized that even though I was doing myself an injustice by wandering into the hands of the enemy and believing every evil, dark thing about the black sheep, in the very depths of my being I was uncomfortable, because I knew what God had chosen me for and had called me to do. It always felt like the Lord was with me. Have you ever been in situations where you knew things were just not right? It's like you knew that you were called to greatness because, no matter what, there was this strong, supernatural force protecting you as you walked around in the world.

Now, I know that as you think things over you can pinpoint a time in your life when you were that black sheep, that misfit, that laughing stock, that outcast, that overlooked person for the job, that forsaken being, that brokenhearted person left to heal on your own, or that person who was abused, yet still you pursued life and never ever spoke up about it. I am speaking to you. If you ever remember anything from this book, remember this, the black sheep experience was for your good. The Bible tells us that all things work out for our good (Romans 8:28). So, even though you and I may experience moments in our lives that resemble the black sheep experience, it is very important that we understand that at the end of every experience, it all works out for the good. The good is you growing to become who God has destined you to be.

   The black sheep experience revealed to me that Jesus is the true Shepherd. As the days turned into nights, as I wandered away doing my own thing, committing sin after sin, His concern grew for me. The Lord is the good Shepherd who continues to seek and search after us. Jesus saw past my flaws and my wandering ways, and He came and found me and brought me back into his sheepfold.

   A sheepfold is a space where sheep are kept when they're not out in the fields. Sheep are usually kept together in the sheepfold, protecting them from danger and harm, such as wolves. The shepherd is in charge of protecting the gate of the sheepfold; a good Shepherd loves and cares for the sheep. He guards and protects them, with His life, against predators. It is his duty to fetch the sheep that stray and leave the fold. The minute I realized that Jesus would continue to search for me every time I left the sheepfold, I realized that despite the many things that have happened to me, good and bad, *the battle was just not mine.*

CHAPTER 8

A.K.A.WOG

It is one thing to be called a 'woman of God,' and it is a totally different thing to just be called a woman. Before God calls you, He usually causes you to go through a process. This goes for both men and women, but in this case, I will speak of how God processed me as a young woman. Whenever someone is asked if they want to give their life to Christ, if they're not ready it is usually followed by, "I am not ready," or "I am not living right, so I can't." But in actuality, Jesus came to save us while we are yet sinners.

    I gave my life to Jesus at a very young age. Many times, people think that when you give your life to Christ at a young age that means you have been in church all your life. But we sin daily, and we acquire new desires as we get older. So, as a young woman, I was not always living, thinking, or walking in the fullness of

God or in the calling on my life. So, yes, this caused me to be just average, and I knew that I was operating as an average woman as well. Deep down in my spirit, I knew that there was an initial call, but I did not want to answer it. So, for a couple of years, I lived my life as an ordinary woman. In other words, I wanted to control everything that happened in my life. Let's not forget that I wanted to work and do regular things, even though God was calling me to extraordinary things and the supernatural. Regular things, for me, were convenient; they didn't require me to do much work. Surely, I know many women can relate to what will be disclosed in this chapter.

So, at this point, you know that I was saved at a very young age and now you know that as I began to grow as a woman I was not walking in the fullness of God but in sin. Sin does not always have to be something sexual, although due to the norm, people think that sexual things are the only sin. Sin is any deed committed wrongfully, knowing full well that you know the truth. So, I was operating illegally as a woman. The reason I can say this now is because, like I said, I wanted control over everything in my life. I was addicted to the love of money. I believed that working and getting money was worth the life I was living. I told many tales—lies—to save myself from many situations. I allowed my emotions to rule who I was instead of allowing God to take care of them. I lived in a lot of fear that was not fair to me, but when fear cripples who you are, only God can truly set you free. Not only did I do all of this, but I was comfortable in the sin, comfortable with allowing men to flirt with me, knowing deep down inside that God would not be pleased with me accepting the smooth mouth of the opposite sex.

This season in my life lasted a very long time, because I was being processed, and this process was very uncomfortable for me. Why? Because it was my will against the Lord's will. The funny thing about it is that I did not see what God was doing until I had no choice but to be in submission to Him. That, of course, did not come easy, because I had situations that would repeat themselves, over and over again. And guess what? I would fail every time. I can remember when I went through a phase in which men would take an interest in me, and I don't mean one or two, but many at a time. I entertained them without having any self-control, entertained the flirt, entertained the conversations that I knew God would not be pleased with. The reason I am sharing this side of my testimony is because I know that many women experience these types of things, but they don't speak about them. The number one reason why women don't speak about their own personal testimonies, if they are anything like mine, is that they want to appear as if they have everything together, or they're afraid of what other people might think. To be honest, that was my problem, but the Bible tells me that we overcome by the words of our testimony. Sharing your testimony is not a bad thing; if anything, it sets you, and many other women that may be in bondage, free.

In the very depths of every young woman's heart are deep secrets that are unspoken, and many painful situations that they refuse to talk about because of how deep they are. So, in the midst of me wanting to take control of everything—my life, my money, my future—deep down it was hurting me. It began to hurt me because there I was doing all the things God should be ruler over. Please believe that I was pushed and tormented. The devil would put me in situations that made me feel less than, and because I just couldn't see it, I would succumb to it every time and fail. When you begin to feel like a failure, that is when the enemy creeps in, and you start to fall for all the silly tricks he places in front of you. It's funny, I was never the type to share any of what was going on with me, because I felt like no one would understand me. This, too, shows that the enemy always enjoys isolating people. Once he has you secluded and isolated from family, friends, and church folk, you become his playground. I struggled with this very thing. Only a few people know my stories as it pertains to this chapter.

My emotions were always broken and

torn, because I had a big heart, I loved deeply, I didn't enjoy seeing people cry, seeing people endure lack, or seeing people sick, so I felt like I was doing God a favour when I tried to help everyone, while the real person who needed the saving grace was me. Naturally, I would place myself on the back burner in hopes of being a superhero for everyone. I just did not realize how much God loved me. I did not turn, neither did I cast my heavy burdens upon Him, as it says in Psalm 55:22—*"Cast your burden on the LORD [release it] and He will sustain and uphold you; He will never allow the righteous to be shaken (slip, fall, fail)."* When you live a carefree life, you get carefree results. The attention that I was receiving by being this ordinary woman was what my flesh desired, so my carefree results came.

Everyone can relate to that satisfying feeling of fulfilling the needs of our flesh. We, as women, do such a good job hiding this issue that sometimes we end up in situations that we don't mean to put ourselves in. For me, I realized that I enjoyed living the smooth life of the ordinary woman, that woman who was average, that woman whom everyone loved, because I controlled everything. It was quite the oxymoron, because God was calling me to be extraordinary and to be set apart when I was not living or walking in the fullness of what He wanted me to be. Believe me when I tell you that I felt so uncomfortable living in sin, it almost felt like God was trying to get my attention, but I was turning down the conviction within me. I would find comfort in believing the lie that was lurking within my heart, yet I knew the Lord was speaking to me, He was telling me I was His prize possession.

Can you imagine being comfortable in your sin? Picture being a slave to sin, succumbing to the things that the devil wants and not what God wants. That is the most controlled feeling there is; you feel like you're being held hostage. It makes you feel like you're on top of the world, but that feeling is temporary. Yes, all of that was me. I endured that average woman mentality, filled with so much power, yet walking around empty, all because I wanted to control my life, all because I wanted to prove something to someone, all because I wanted to save the world as a woman, only to end up losing every battle there was as a young woman. Then one day, God began to do something on the inside of me, this time it didn't resemble the work of the enemy. God began to shake up some things in my life as a young woman. Not only that, but I also began to reach out to God like never before, because I was thirsty; not the thirst for control that I wanted to have, but the thirst that only God could quench. John 7:37-39 says, *"On the last day, the climax of the festival, Jesus stood and shouted to the crowds, 'Anyone who is thirsty may come to me! Anyone who believes in me may come and drink! For the Scriptures declare, 'Rivers of living water will flow from his heart." (When he said "living water," he was speaking of the Spirit, who would be given to everyone believing in him. But the Spirit had not yet been given, because Jesus had not yet entered into his glory.)'"* This passage fed my spirit every time I read it, yet I didn't know why God was bringing me to this scripture. I didn't know why He wanted to quench this fleshly thirst that I had for the things of the world.

The money, the control, and the ability to use charm just weren't cutting it anymore as a woman. The average woman just wasn't cutting it anymore. Time after time, I would struggle to get through the days, the weeks, and the months, all because I was so busy wanting control. Having control is so much easier than giving it to someone else. But, you know, this all got me nowhere. It only caused my spirit to be uncomfortable because, deep inside, there was that dividing factor, that thing that separated me from doing what God beckoned my heart to do. Truthfully, I was living a life of lies, pretending to be okay, yet deep down inside I had displaced issues, a brokenness that only a woman could understand, wanting a sense of belonging that I knew I just would never ever get. All these things set me back.

Did I mention that during this time I was attending Sunday morning services, Sunday after Sunday? Well, I was, and I sure know many women wake up and do the same thing. I applied the flashy make up from MAC, Sephora, or some other high-end brand, the flashy red lipstick or that famous heroine colour, come on, you once did this if you're a woman. It really took someone who was able to see through me to realize that I was not walking in the fullness of God. So, yes, that side of me had a form of godliness but not the power of God.

Still, I was thirsty for God. As I became thirsty for Him, I realized that He truly wanted to quench the thirst I had for the things of this world. To be honest, I just didn't know how He was going to do it, I didn't know where he was going to start and, most importantly, I didn't know how I was going to look when He dealt with this part of my life as a woman. Yet, for some strange reason, I felt a peace come over me that passed all understanding. No longer was I worried about what people would think, neither was I afraid to give up my control. Now, I am sure you're wondering how the process started. It started when I recognized that my sinful behaviours and actions were contrary to what God required of me as a woman. Then I began to genuinely pray to God. I asked Him to help me as I was willing to go through this process alone, for Him to make me over and transform me into the woman of God that He wanted me to be. So, day after day and night after night, I would start off by praying specific prayers to Him. Many of them were very embarrassing to pray because of how far gone I actually was in my sinfulness. Tears would flow every time. I knew that I needed Him to purge me and deliver me from this controlling spirit that wanted to literally deter me from the blessings and the fullness God wanted for me.

As I prayed these specific prayers, I realized that I felt a warm feeling consuming me whenever I spent time in the presence of God. So because I loved the experience and, of course, because I needed to be changed and delivered, I would constantly spend time telling God that I did not like the person I had become and that I wanted to be completely transformed, not just in appearance but in speech and in dress. Be careful what you pray for because, I kid you not, that prayer was answered.

The Lord began to deal with me. He started with my insides, making sure that my heart matched my word, especially if I was going to be His vessel. Then he proceeded to guide my tongue, because I used to say whatever came to my lips. I didn't know that the reason He changed and moved my heart first was because everything originates from the heart, things that come out thereafter proceed from the mouth. Then He started to change my mind. There was a certain amount of control that the enemy would have over my mind, until I literally had to seek God to help me guard my mind and help me think positively and not negatively. I realized that I was being disciplined in thought so that I could reflect Christ. This entire transformation—mind, body, and soul—was an uncomfortable one. It caused me to, at times, second guess when God was speaking to me, but at the same time, it taught me to hear the voice of God.

Now, the reason why I say all of this is because Proverbs 31 tells me that a woman of God, or a worthy woman, is one who flows and operates differently than the ordinary woman. According to Scripture, a woman of God is someone who is an encourager, who is spiritual, intelligent, trustworthy, hardworking, a cook, a wise business woman, strong, bold, wise, unique, and who fears the Lord. Many times, I told God that I wanted to demonstrate these character traits, not knowing that that was His initial goal for me. So, now that God allowed me to go through the process of being a woman who was ordinary and average to being a woman of God (W.O.G.), God let me know through this process that my character had to represent Him and not the world, and that if I slipped or fell there would be consequences surrounding my decisions and my actions. Despite the pain of letting go, I traded wanting my own way, I traded the brokenness, the pain, the unforgiveness, the love of money, and the unwanted flirtatious conversations that I would entertain as an average woman, I traded it all in for a true lifestyle of having Jesus Christ.

Despite how I felt and how much control I wanted over situations and things, the Lord truly humbled me. He allowed me to see the good and the bad, and disciplined me in these areas. He increased my discernment through it all, because He wanted me to hear His voice on how to represent Him as a true woman of God. I learned some hard lessons as the Lord began to process me into a woman of God. I cried many tears during the night, because the desire would creep in, ever so often, to revert to being regular old me. But even that was a lesson that I had to learn, and the interesting thing is that I would find myself in repetitive situations, learning the same lesson, not once, not twice, but three or more times. It gave me a godly sorrow that caused me to really look into myself. It caused me to stand back for a second and ask myself how much I wanted to be a true representation of Christ.

When I realized that I truly had no control over my situations, that was when I surrendered. It's funny that things need to happen before we truly surrender to God, especially if we're trying to follow Him and pursue Him in every area of our lives. As a woman, I realized that in order to follow my destiny, in order to live a life of freedom, I had to let go of being that ordinary woman, that average woman, that woman of control. It was when I let go and let God that I realized that my pride and my will were no longer in my hands but in the hands of the Lord. It was then that I realized that this battle, even *this battle, was not mine*.

CHAPTER 9

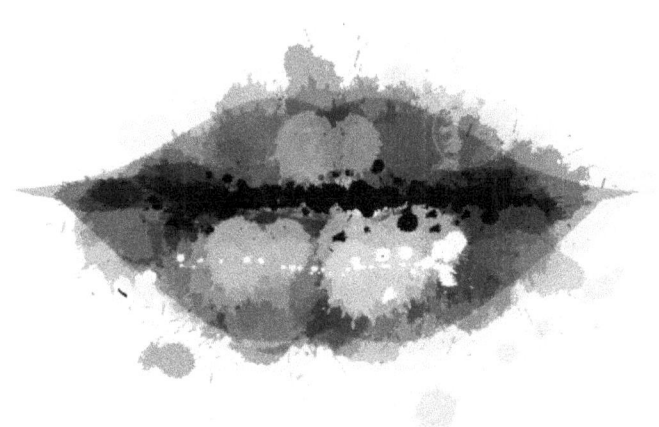

Secretly Bruised Behind Ministry

Have you ever noticed that when you get cut or bruised there's always a reaction of some sort? I want you to imagine, for just one moment, jamming your finger or even stubbing your toe on the edge of a wall. Picture how painful it is. That first reaction probably sounded like "Ouch!" "Darn it!" or even a scream followed by tears. If you're anything like me, it would be the last option, especially if it truly hurt. However, at the end of the day, it had to hurt you in order to heal. There is a process after receiving a cut—first it bleeds, thereafter is the drying of the wound or the healing of the bruise. So, again I say, a cut or bruise has to hurt you in order to heal you.

Now that you have gotten the revelation, I will go further to explain in hopes of helping you understand that every situation that was meant to hurt you and me was meant to bring healing to our wounds. This chapter will expose the things that people like me encounter but keep a closed mouth about. This chapter is meant to enlighten those who do not know that those who follow Christ do suffer for His name's sake. Those who are called into ministry are not perfect; we are far from it. However, when the Lord handpicks and chooses you to accomplish His specific assignment, there is a reason. Within that reason is warfare, growing pains, tragic deaths, criticism, jealousy from other ministers running in the same race as you, the likelihood of being overlooked for opportunities, and bitterness in the hearts of men because one person might operate differently in their anointing. At the end of the day, everyone's ministry is not the same, and the path that they have to walk is not the same. Although it may seem similar, each person's journey is different.

    My journey doing the ministry that I believe God has placed within me has been a very interesting one, one that doesn't resemble the next woman or man. Earlier in the book I mentioned that I experienced many different things that caused me to know that God was on my side and that I was without a shadow of a doubt called to be a minister for Him. However, there was always restriction, always growing pains that I had to experience, both personally and spiritually. Anyone who is a true minister of God is running in a race where there are constant hurdles that need to be jumped over in order to see the grand prize. Ministry is something that I always took seriously, because someone is waiting for you and me to show them some sort of light at the end of their dark tunnel. At times, I would find myself dying to myself so that the work of the Lord could be accomplished.

For those ministers who can relate, they know the importance of burning that midnight oil, receiving late night phone calls for the sake of ministry, having to prepare to bury family members, friends, and perfect strangers, then turning around and conducting weddings, holding prayer conferences, crusades, and conventions, all to make sure that they're fulfilling the true calling of God. Many of the roles I just listed are done by those who preach, prophesy, or pastor. But there are also those who work in the background, the ones whom God has chosen to carry forth His will. Many people know these individuals as the ones who sing, dance, write, play instruments, just to name a few. These same people are in a holding pattern; they're waiting, wanting God to use them for His glory and for His kingdom, but they're overlooked. They're always told, "You're not ready," yet those who are already in ministry are afraid to teach them. One thing I know is that the Bible tells me about two people, Elijah and Elisha. When Elijah's time was up, his successor was Elisha. It takes two to accomplish anything.

My experience in ministry has been one centred on constant rejection, both openly and privately. I don't speak on these things to make anyone feel sorry for me or to pinpoint any one thing that may have led up to this chapter of my book. However, I have chosen to encourage those who are experiencing hurt when they're chosen for this thing called ministry.

As a young girl, as mentioned in a previous chapter, I was always different, but I didn't know that my different and God's different had two separate meanings. My different meant that I didn't do what others did, and if I did, I would do it in a creative way. Then, as I grew and understood my walk with the Lord more, I realized that His different meant purpose. He wanted to fulfill His purpose for my life. He would constantly show me visions of myself in buildings, sharing my testimony and encouraging women and men who went through similar things as I did. However, when I answered His call and said yes to ministry, I did not know that I would get bruised, used, and abused for the sake of ministry. There were times when I would feel such a big heart towards the Body of Christ that I just wanted to encourage others through the talents and gifts that the Lord had given me. Unfortunately, there was always someone there to tell me that I was not ready. They would block me from opportunities every time. Many nights I would cry and tell God that I no longer wanted to be in ministry, I no longer wanted to participate, I no longer wanted to help this "Kingdom" that was so wicked and cruel to me. My heart was so passionate about this thing called ministry that I would find myself trying to hop back on the wagon of ministry again, helping, praying for, and encouraging others. Yet, there was always a resistance with every opportunity that presented itself that God had given me the go-ahead to try.

My family and certain friends saw the ministry within me, yet even they would ask me, "Janice, what are you doing with yourself? When is the album coming out? When are we going to hear what God has placed inside of your heart?"

With absolute shock, I would say, "Whenever God is ready." Or sometimes I would just reply with a shy "I know."

But no one was there to truly say, "Janice, come let me teach you, come and let me show you."

That was a bruise that was always being hit with words and with actions from those who possibly knew my potential but were afraid to help me. I was afraid as well, because I knew what God was saying to me but didn't know how or what to do to get there. So, guess what I did? I went around asking people to help me or even just suggest some things I could do as a young minister coming up. Why did I do that? Well, like I said, Elijah had a successor named Elisha, so I believe that when a young minister is coming up, he or she should have some type of guidance. Now, when I say guidance, I don't mean control, neither do I mean that you should be thrown out to swim with the sharks just like that, because there is a process when ministry is involved. To my surprise, everyone that I went to either ignored me, did not get back to me, or started to help me and then withdrew the help without telling me why. That is the most hurtful feeling anyone can experience. Nevertheless, I say this to say that many ministers, and I don't just mean those who have a title in front of their names, but ministers of music, dance, and the creative arts have experienced this.

Unfortunately, we live in a world where those who have titles are usually the most recognized, and those who just might be the next successors are overlooked due to too many ministers not discerning when their time is up. Now, please read this in the sincerest tone, it was never about titles for me. I couldn't care less because, at the end of the day, we will be judged by God according to our relationship with Him and how we treated others. The aid of mentorship was something I would have appreciated, but it never came. I know not everyone knows Christ, but I am sure you can relate to what I am saying—wanting someone to mentor you but though they see the potential in you to be great, they have no time to push you into greatness. The process of going through this growing pain felt like it was never going to end.

Imagine having to always prove yourself in church choirs and worship teams, and imagine having the ability to speak or preach in front of people, only to hear that you're not ready. In the corporate world, when someone is not ready after being trained, they usually offer that person extra training, so that they're able to do the job. For me, there were all of these promises to train and none of them ever came. It bothered me to the point where I gave up. I stopped asking, I stopped inquiring, I stopped reaching out to everyone, because I felt like I was a waste of time to every single person I encountered.

Another area that ministers experience being bruised are those moments that absolutely no one but God sees, the praying and the fasting, which increases your relationship with God and His anointing on your life. When someone is anointed, it just means that they have been selected by God and not man. For some strange reason, there are people who think that your anointing is up for sale. There are even people who become jealous of you and the anointing that you carry but have no idea what you had to go through to keep it, much less attain it. Many ministers go through this and say absolutely nothing. The journey for me, and the anointing that God Himself gave to me, has been a rollercoaster. I say this because what's in this book does not compare to what I have gone through. Therefore, I encourage every single person who is a minister of the gospel and who has read up to this point that you're not alone.

I know many nights you may wonder, "Can I endure this? All this?" Yes, you sure can. Think about how Jesus endured the cross; He went without a murmur. Just continue to allow God to be your strength, strength like no other. Believe it or not, the bruises that I received while in ministry have caused me to grow, to shed tears, to say, "I give up," to feel low, to get up and try again, to repent and tell God, "Sorry for rejecting what you've placed inside of me." So, if you're being silent while enduring the wounds, the bruises, when people talk about you and tell lies on you, I can relate.

There were times I would cry without my own family even knowing what ministry in the church had done to me. Sometimes I would go days without eating, because I felt so moved, because of the many times my character was spoken badly about. Only God in Heaven could save me from walking away from ministry and His will altogether. But God.

When you're experiencing the bruises and the wounds, I know at times it feels like you're alone, but believe me, you're never alone. God is with you, and you can be sure that someone is going through a similar situation. God allowed me to come to the realization that in ministry you die daily, because ministry is a selfless walk. One day I told God, "You know what, God, no matter what is said about me, good or bad, I know that you fight all my battles."

The Lord says in His Word that He never leaves us nor forsakes us. The minute I grasped that concept about ministry, He gave me so much more confidence, boldness, and courage to accept the fact that silent bruises and wounds are all a part of the process. I also knew that this experience, *this battle, was not mine* to win.

CHAPTER 10

Leave the Boat

In life, there are many decisions that need to be made for the betterment of our lives. Not only that, but we have decisions that require us to define our faith and why we are living on this earth. Then, there are decisions that require us to risk some things and possibly even risk it all. At the end of the day, these decisions require us to jump out of the boat; it is only then that we will know our true value, our true destiny, and what we can accomplish in life. I can vividly recall Matthew 14:28-31, which says, *"Then Peter called to him, 'Lord, if it's really you, tell me to come to you, walking on the water.' 'Yes, come,' Jesus said. So Peter went over the side of the boat and walked on the water toward Jesus. But when he saw the strong wind and the waves, he was terrified and began to sink. 'Save me,*

Lord!' he shouted. Jesus immediately reached out and grabbed him. 'You have so little faith,' Jesus said. 'Why did you doubt me?'" This passage expresses how important it is to have faith in Jesus, not just in some things, but in all things. As you're going through life's trials and boisterous storms, when you have decisions to make but you can't hear from God, know that He cares for you, know that He will prove Himself to you, if He has not already done so. The disciples in this part of the Book of Matthew were very timid. Peter, however, was eager to jump out of the boat to see if he could also walk on water. It was his faith in Jesus that allowed him to walk on the water the way Jesus did. The minute he took his eyes off Jesus, he began to sink.

Believe it or not, distractions can cause us to miss God. You might ask, "How?" Well, a distraction is anything that interferes with your ability to focus on something. One of the problems I had was focusing on the will of God, focusing on His face and His voice whenever He would speak to me and show up in my life. Just like Peter who walked on the water and got distracted, the distractions and doubts that I had came when I wanted to control the direction of my life, when I wanted to follow the wrong crowd instead of standing out. This caused me to miss God. As the strong and boisterous winds tossed me around, they would blow me from one bad opportunity to the next, from one stressful situation to the next, they caused me to be worrisome about my future and to turn down my destiny as it pertained to God and His will. During this time, fear grew so big inside of me that when an opportunity presented itself I would run away or I would downplay what God had blessed me with to share with others for His glory. So, there I was chaining myself to this life boat, this boat that God wanted me to step out of, like Peter. I did everything to stay in the boat, not knowing that God wanted me to taste and see that He is good. It was comfortable inside the boat. I didn't have to put in the work, nor did I have to encounter the warfare that would possibly come at me if I jumped out of the boat. That, ladies and gentlemen, was a clear sign that God was not the controller of my life, rather fear of doing what He told me to do was. So, I was stagnant in the boat, not wanting to step out of my comfort zone. A comfort zone is any place that feels comfortable, a place that literally has no meaning because you're stagnant, doing nothing. I complained all the time about my situation to my family and friends, but I never tried Jesus by jumping out of the boat and taking a risk in Jesus' name. There I was, weathering the storm, unlike Peter who wanted to go. I was okay with not putting God to the test. The boisterous winds nearly killed me. In this chapter a boisterous wind can be any distraction in your life. These distractions, if we set our minds on them, can devour us.

This boat of mine consisted of many things that were weighing me down. One day I sat down and thought about it, just me and God. God knew the posture of my heart at this time, because there was a desire to put my best foot forward but, for some reason, I was always downplaying the confidence I had built up in God. This caused me to stay in the boat. Many times, I would put my foot up on the edge of the boat to jump out and walk towards the Lord's direction concerning my life, but there was always some enticing opportunity far off in the distance. Therefore, instead of going in the Lord's direction, the pretty, shiny, sparkly new opportunity that came up would cause me to put my foot back inside the boat, lingering in a stagnant situation, again. I don't know if you've ever experienced that feeling before, wanting to run to God but your flesh causes you to stay, then you end up missing God due to your own wants.

This boat experience, and wanting to trust God in the midst of all the noise, caused me to truly evaluate my life. It was either I get dragged away by the devil, or submit to the will of God and allow Him to make me feel liberated and free in Jesus' name. However, this would only be through me taking a risk and trusting Him with my future and the ministry goals that He put inside me. Now, the boat can be defined as any place in your life that may be comfortable or familiar to you, in which there is no growth, just cycles that replay themselves, over and over again, causing you to not take a leap of faith. Jumping out of what is familiar and comfortable is the part I feared.

It's interesting that Peter and I had many similarities but also many differences. The one thing that we did not have in common was the courage to want to jump. Peter taught me that in order to take a risk you have to dare yourself to take that risk. Peter dared to leave the boat to see if it was truly Jesus who was walking upon the water. The funny thing about this is that if he didn't take courage, or have a willingness to jump out and leave all that was familiar, including the disciples that looked on, he would not have been able to say that he was the only person daring enough to put God to the test. I was not so daring, because I didn't have that drive to jump out of the boat and trust God.

Keep in mind that even before I actually jumped—because eventually I did jump—my entire body reacted. Likewise, many things will cause your body to react to jumping out of the boat, you may even panic about the decision to jump and allow God to have His way. I am sure you're wondering to yourself, "When did Janice say yes to jumping out of the boat like Peter did?" Well, the desire to jump wasn't there, but I had to just do it. It literally was the only thing left to do. When I no longer wanted to stay in the boat, when I felt like the boat was getting too small for me, that was when I realized that it was time to take some risks in my personal life in terms of trusting Jesus. Not only that, but God allowed the boat that I was in to be shaken, and when I say shaken, I mean everything around me stopped making sense, certain desires got shaken, taken away until I submitted to the will of the Father. But, of course, me being me, before I jumped I said a prayer to Jesus.

I said, "Jesus, if you desire for my life to go a specific way, which is obviously your way, please be my safety net. I know that I've allowed my fear and disbelief to cause me to submit to my own will and desires, but if you desire for me to follow your will and your way, if you have more for me, please prove it to me in some way, and I will trust you with my life and everything taking place in it."

The minute I said this honest prayer, God began to do the remarkable. It was then that I jumped out of the boat. When I jumped, I was scared, but then I realized that He wanted to give me more, He wanted to do more for me than what I wanted or could do for myself. Things began to happen supernaturally, help came from all areas. When I was lacking and in need, and I mean truly in need, God showed up.

You will never know what awaits you out there in the deep, especially when it has to do with the things of God concerning your life, unless you jump. So, if you are in a situation where you are contemplating jumping out of the boat, my godly advice to you is to jump. Believe me, the Lord will catch you. He will reach His hands out and He will be your safety net in the most destructive experiences, the scariest of times, the most lacking of times, the most hurtful times, the times that no one knows about but Him. He will catch you, but you must first take the jump, the leap of faith, so that He can meet you at the well. You will never know your true potential in Christ if you continue to neglect His voice when He tells you to jump out of the boat. Like I said, if I did not listen to His voice and allow Him to do this work within me, I would still be in the boat. It was through my personal relationship that I realized that stepping out of the boat required me to know Him and to hearken to His voice. It was when I jumped out of the boat, leaving fear, hurt, disbelief, pain, worry, doubt, and everything that hindered me that I realized that this, my brothers and sisters, *this battle was not mine.*

CHAPTER 11

The Battle Is For His Glory

It is important to know when you are in warfare. It makes no sense for a solider to show up for battle yet not know whom he's up against or what he's up against. So, for the true believers who believe in the true and living God, it is important to know who and what we are up against. Our battles may look like we're up against all odds—bill collectors calling our homes constantly due to unpaid bills or missed promises to pay; out-of-control family members not acting right; job situations that just don't seem to align themselves with the direction of your goals or are not as stable as you once thought they would have been. It almost feels and looks like everything is shaky. Heating and electricity bills cause you to worry, wondering where your next meal is coming from and how the rent or mortgage is going to get paid. Let's not forget to mention when family members and friends pass away, and the battle of having to heal from not having them around anymore seems impossible to handle. All of these things are battles that we face daily, plus others. The beauty of being on the battlefield for the Lord is that once we begin to realize that the battle does not belong to us, we will realize that we have someone fighting for us behind the scenes, if only we would be still in the midst of the battle.

The reason I decided to write about this in this particular chapter is that I've noticed that many people are going through their own secret battles. What we need to understand in our battles is that, according to Ephesians 6:12 (NLT), *"We are not fighting against flesh-and-blood enemies, but against evil rulers and authorities of the unseen world, against mighty powers in this dark world, and against evil spirits in the heavenly places."* The battles that we face are a lot deeper than what we might think. So when we think it is a person, place, or thing, in actuality it is not flesh and blood, it is spiritual darkness, the things that we can't see. For example, throughout this entire book I've shared some personal things that I had to go through in order to have a testimony. I am no different from you; we all have our own battles that we fight daily. Some of my battles were repetitive, because I tried to fight the battle, the plan, or the will of God instead of letting Him fight my battles for me. Through this, I realized that in order for us, as soldiers of Christ, to succeed at any battle in our lives, we must allow the Lord to fight our battles for us. It is also the same thing when we have battles happening within our flesh.

In my own strength, I lost every battle, hence the title of this book, *The Battle Was Not Mine*. During every single battle that presented itself to me, I realized that God wanted me to take comfort in Him and His divine victory that He was setting up for me. Have you ever noticed that when a solider is getting ready for a fight that he prepares his armour, his shield, and makes sure he's fully protected? Well, as I think things over, I realize that I was not protected, because I was fighting my own issues and problems without any protection, saying small prayers in hopes of having my way with everything, but that was not God's will for my life. Thus, the battles of being teased, spat upon, beaten up, called hurtful names, being bullied, the battle of wanting to be accepted by man, not knowing that I was already pre-approved by God, the battle of rejection everywhere I went, the battle of being an average woman, the experience of God processing me into a woman of God, and the battle of my own fleshy, secret desires was all a part of God's plan. With that being said, if you're at a place in your life where you, too, are experiencing battle after battle, and you just don't want to let go and allow Jesus Christ, the soon coming King to handle it, eventually He will take full control over the direction of your life, and He will send all the right people while you're being tossed around, refusing to give up to Him.

For those of you who are battling with the voice of the Lord and who this Jesus Christ person is, all it takes is one experience to see that God is trying to get your attention. When you have an encounter with the Creator, you will begin to understand who He is and, even then, it will be a wonder for you, because it will be an encounter you probably have never had before. The point I am trying to make is that this life brings battles that we sometimes have no control over, but how we react in battle can make a big impact on the onlooker. In this case, I hope you picking up this book to read what I have shared from my heart has caused you to evaluate the battles you are facing in your life, so that you will someday give them to God. A battle can be any issue you are facing that you just cannot get out of because of how hard it is to fight in your own strength. My battles are different than your battles, but the moral of the story is that no battle, no drug addiction, no sex addiction, no lust, no spirit of perversion, no stealing, no low self-esteem, no pain, no divorce, no lost loved one, no homosexual spirit, no lack of finances, no brokenness, no broken marriage, no miscarriage, no lost job, no lost house, no lost car, no molestation, no rape, no disability, no jail sentence, no broken family, none of these battles are a secret to the Lord Jesus Christ. He knows and He wants you to allow Him to fight these battles that you try to handle on your own, in your heart, in your secret place that absolutely no one knows about. It is in these times that God tries to get our attention, and I encourage you to no longer turn down His voice while you go through your battles. Please refrain from doing it like me. I wrote this book to encourage you through my own battles, which are a big deal because the Lord has fought every single one of them. So please, don't learn the hard way like I had to. Don't be stubborn to His voice, for His voice is still. Don't get me wrong, I am not perfect and neither are you. Yes, the battles will continuously come and, yes, the weapons will form, but the Bible says that no weapon formed against you or me shall prosper.

Every battle that I had to endure was because God wanted to fight it for me, but I just didn't want to get over my flesh and allow Him to fight. It has been a very long time coming, but I would not trade it for anything in this world, because I can see the hand of God in my life more now since I gave up my will and traded it to Him. I encourage you to try His will. Let go and let God fight your battles, for every battle is the Lord's, it is not yours, neither is it mine. Oftentimes, we feel that we have the power to change a situation, person, place, or thing, but if it is not God's will, we will bump our heads trying to be the world changer. Believe me, the Lord always prepared a way when there was a battle ahead of me. I remember the times when I wouldn't have to fight my enemies when they came up against me because God knew what He was trying to do in me. All of this was character building; the battles changed my character, because if I were to tell you that I was like this all my life that would be a full-blown lie. So, for every battle that I, Janice Codling, had to go through up to this point, I have seen the hand of the Lord in my life, and for this I am thankful.

He is a loving God who died for all of my struggles and even my defeats. I am so thankful to have traded in my will for His will. And as I continue on in this race, as I stand on the battlefield, I am filled with joy, knowing that I no longer have to fight for my freedom in my own strength. I no longer have to settle for less, no longer have to give into my desires, and I no longer have to pretend to fight a battle that I know I will never win in my own strength, because, ladies and gentlemen, boys and girls, preachers, apostles, prophets, pastors, evangelists, and teachers, I can truly say that *the battle was not mine!*

Your battle, my battle, is for the glory of God to be seen through us and for His name to be lifted up in the earth.

CHAPTER 12

The Best Is Yet to Come

Anytime you hear about a battle following suit, it is one of two things—a victory or a defeat. In this case, the battle that I am speaking about is the battle that you may have going on in your own personal world. You know that world of yours that absolutely no one knows about? That battle. If you think about it for one second, a battle pretty much makes up smaller components of a bigger picture, and it usually happens between two things— two people, two armies, or a struggle within oneself. However, after every battle there is either victory or defeat, so after every internal or external battle you will either win or lose. Once you've turned over any spiritual battle to God, you must stand in wait, knowing and trusting that God will fight for you and that He will win.

After you have fully given up your battles to the Lord, there is an aftermath. The aftermath is the victory. When I gave the Lord all of these battles that I had going on internally and externally, I realized that He wanted to fight them and win them just for me. When my victory came, I was amazed. My victory came when I realized that certain things didn't bother me as much anymore, because I allowed the Lord to handle the internal side first and then the external. This allowed me to no longer live in fear of what others might think of me. God gave me victory over my self-esteem, because I was always picked on and bullied for no reason, which caused me to feel small and look small among people. When I told God that I needed Him to help me get through it, as opposed to fighting the battle on my own, He helped me stand stronger, and victory was mine.

When the battles were over and the Lord caused me to win, the Lord caused me to sit very pretty in the midst of my enemies and caused me to become victorious. It was then that I realized that the best was yet to come. In the natural, after an army finishes with a battle, there is always a cleanup. Many dead bodies of fallen soldiers are picked up and disposed of and, of course, the location of the battle is left in ruins. As it is in the natural, so it is in the spiritual. You see, when I allowed the

Lord to fight my battles, there was a clean up process that the Lord did in the spiritual. When He cleans you up, He performs His makeover, causing you to learn that you cannot fight these earthly battles, these personal battles, and these spiritual battles on your own. Since God is victorious over our battles, He allows us to be at our best through His victory. The result of this victory will cause you to sit before great men and women of God. He causes favour to find you when you know you truly don't deserve it. If you doubt what I am saying to you, I urge you to give it a try, give the Lord every battle you're facing, and if He comes through for you that will be your living proof that He is indeed real.

When I no longer suffered from the opinions of others, God allowed me to see who He is in my life. He granted access to things that I should have been denied access to. When I should have been six feet under, He turned the entire situation around the minute I trusted Him for healing. The minute I feared him and not man, boldness and power became my being. The moment I gave up my will, He replaced it with His perfect will.

Now, don't get me wrong, many will think, "Oh, Janice makes this sound so easy." I will tell you this, it will not be easy, because you will constantly be tested. Let's not forget that Jesus Himself was tested, but He made up His mind that He was on a mission for the Father, and

He did not want anything to deter that. No, we are not Jesus, we are human beings and we are not perfect, but we all have decisions that we must make. If you are not quite sure where you stand right now, know that it is never too late to want to know who Jesus Christ is.

My victory came when I submitted to Jesus, when I gave Him my all. I had many questions in my mind, including *Will Jesus truly fight my battles? Will He truly cover and protect me? Will He still love me for having these thoughts?* And Jesus would always tell me that yes, He would. His Word tells me that He will never leave me nor forsake me; that alone was good enough for me to take a chance and allow Him to fight my battles for me. His glory began to be seen in me, because I allowed Him to have His way with me. I was no longer fighting to have my own way, all of that was out the door. The growth is only painful when you force yourself not to grow in Him. The best was yet to come for me.

Believe it or not, sometimes we hold up our own best-is-yet-to-come moments because we want our way instead of His ways. We hold up our own blessings when we put our hands in the midst of what God is trying to do. I knew that it was either I become my own victim or I allow God to make me a victor. So I gave it all up just so the Lord could have His own way in me. I realized that my strength ran out, playing hide-and-go-seek with God when it was convenient ended, beating up myself for being vulnerable, broken, defeated, oppressed, and depressed was all over when I said, "Lord, the battle is not mine, but yours!"

Jesus Christ took me and cleaned me up. He allowed me to shine in the most horrible times of my life. Even when others counted me out, God just kept on keeping His words and His promises towards me. He knew what He was doing, and it sure didn't look like anything I had in mind. As He began to clean me up and make me new, He allowed others to see my strengths instead of my weaknesses, my smile instead of my frown, my joy instead of my tears and, most of all, His light that He wanted to shine through me. After all these battles, and after the warfare that I had to encounter, all He said to me was, "My daughter, just endure. It may be painful, but just endure." Through these words, I realized that God had a plan, and His plan was to give me the best. Although life may constantly be a battle, Jesus lets me know that the warrior within me will never die as long as I let Him fight my battles for me, because, after all, the battle was not mine.

If you're facing a battle or you are experiencing a high level of warfare, the best thing to do is submit them to Jesus. Now, I know that many who read this book may not be born again or know who Jesus Christ is, but once upon a time I didn't know who He is either. However, through experiencing the good, the bad, and the ugly, I realized that there truly has to be a God who keeps saving me from all these battles, when every single one of them should have taken me out of this world. My advice to you, if I may, is to try Jesus. Stop fighting your battles today and give Him a chance to bring you into your best-is-yet-to-come moment. I guarantee that you, too, will be able to say, "Janice was correct. Truly *the battle was not mine* but the Lord's!"

www.ingramcontent.com/pod-product-compliance
Lightning Source LLC
Chambersburg PA
CBHW070504100426
42743CB00010B/1752